SECONDARY STARTERS
AND PLENARIES
GEOGRAPHY

Ready-to-use activities for teaching geography

By Brin Best and Steve Padget

BLOOMSBURY

LONDON • NEW DELHI • NEW YORK • SYDNEY

Published 2014 by Bloomsbury Education
Bloomsbury Publishing plc
50 Bedford Square, London, WC1B 3DP

www.bloomsbury.com

9-781-4411-1091-6
© Brin Best and Steve Padget 2014

A CIP record for this publication is available from the British Library.

10 9 8 7 6 5 4 3 2 1

Typeset by Fakenham Prepress Solutions, Fakenham, Norfolk NR21 8NN
Printed by CPI Group (UK) Ltd, Croydon, CR0 4YY

This book is produced using paper that is made from wood grown in managed, sustainable forests. It is natural, renewable and recyclable. The logging and manufacturing processes conform to the environmental regulations of the country of origin.

To view more of our titles please visit www.bloomsbury.com

Online resources accompany this book and are available at:

www.bloomsbury.com/secondary-starters-and-plenaries-geography-9781441110916

Please type the URL into your web browser and follow the instructions to access the resources. If you experience any problems, please contact Bloomsbury at: companionwebsite@bloomsbury.com

Contents

Section 10: Geographical reflection

157

Acknowledgements

We would like to express our thanks to the following people who have made important contributions to this book.

Kathryn Needham, former Sustainable Transport Officer for the Yorkshire Dales National Park Authority, contributed the entry 'Connecting rural communities sustainably', which included liaison with the current staff involved in the project to bring the case study fully up to date. We also thank Louise Fountain, Head of Trading at Attenborough Nature Centre (Nottinghamshire Wildlife Trust) and Matt Jackson, Head of Conservation Strategy at the Berks, Bucks and Oxon Wildlife Trust for their help with Starter/Plenary 'Looking after the local environment'; Ollie Padget, D.Phil student in animal behaviour, for information and guidance given for the construction of Starter/Plenary 'Living with conservation'; and Emma Lockley, Marine Mammal Observer, Gardline Marine Services, for valuable support with Starter/Plenary 'Why "dolphin friendly" fishing'.

Holly Gardner, our editor at Bloomsbury, provided valuable support as we endeavoured to make the book as useful as possible to geography teachers. We are also grateful for the faith she has shown in us throughout the project.

Brin Best

I would like to express my gratitude for the guidance and support provided by Bob Hordern, former Head of Geography at Settle High School, North Yorkshire. My distinctive philosophy for the teaching of geography had its roots in the four years working with Bob, who is without doubt the most expert geography teacher I have worked with. I am also indebted to the hundreds of pupils who entered into the creative spirit I tried to offer in my geography lessons, allowing me to explore possibilities of the subject. Research for this book required me to travel extensively across the country in search of interesting case studies, and in every destination I had to find somewhere comfortable to write. I am particularly grateful in this context to the staff of Bewley's Hotel, Leeds and for the splendid library area available at this fine hotel. I would also like to thank the friendly baristas from the numerous Costa and Starbucks coffee shops where I sought refuge and found a warm welcome, freshly brewed coffee and free Wi-Fi. Finally, I want to offer special thanks to my wife Amanda for her unfailing support during the writing of this book. Beyond this support, I could not have wished for a better companion with which to share so many geographical wonders.

Steve Padget

To the many people who have helped, inspired and contributed to the construction of this book, my thanks are due. In particular, I would like to acknowledge the inspiration given to me over the years of my teaching career by John Eaton, my geography teacher at Northgate Grammar School, Ipswich. I would also like to acknowledge the boundless help, support and inspiration of Julie, Ollie and Becky – the home team.

Introduction

The aim of this book is to bring excitement and high levels of engagement to your geography lessons, so that your pupils feel really inspired by the subject. We want your pupils to leave your lessons feeling exhilarated about what they have learnt and eager to return to your classroom for more. And we want the geography department to be known across the school as the place where the most interesting lessons take place.

These high expectations for what you can achieve in your classroom with the help of this book are built on the many successes of our own award-winning departments, and the work of numerous geography teachers across the country – from NQTs to highly experienced teachers – whose lessons we have observed. Through these examples we know that it *is* possible to achieve impressive results in your classroom *every day*, to have pupils regularly thank you for a great lesson and for the buzz of geography to permeate the whole school. This book will help you to achieve all these things – and more.

The central role of starters and plenaries in geography lessons

A wealth of education research has been published that backs up the assertion that the most effective learning in geography consists of distinctive *learning episodes* where pupils are made to *think deeply and incisively* about the subject matter, working alone and with others to *mesh new learning into their existing knowledge frameworks*. Starters and plenaries are a particularly powerful tool for teachers because they offer wonderful opportunities for knowledge acquisition, incisive pupil thinking and skill development during short, discrete learning episodes that nevertheless can have long-lasting effects.

This book contains a wealth of learning opportunities in the form of 50 engaging starters and plenaries that can be used with minimal preparation but with maximum impact. The entries deal with a very wide range of topics taken from the modern geography curriculum, and include several that focus on pupil skills.

We are convinced that the very best starters and plenaries in geography have several characteristics in common, and we have used these as the basis for designing all the entries in this book. These features, which should be borne in mind as you deliver the starters and plenaries and when you use your creativity to devise your own, are outlined below.

High quality starters and plenaries usually share the following six characteristics:

- They help pupils develop their geographical knowledge and/or skills by focusing mainly on one *discrete area* of the curriculum.

- They help pupils to understand important *geographical principles* that can be applied in a variety of contexts.

- They encourage pupils to *think deeply* about geographical topics and case studies, and ask *relevant questions*.

- They help pupils make *links* between different aspects of the subject through knowledge- or skills-bridges*.

- They provide pupils with deep geographical learning that they can take with them beyond their formal schooling.

- They provide a means of addressing the themes of the Global Dimension and Sustainable Development, and therefore make a meaningful contribution to the school's work on two important cross-curricular themes.

Defining the curriculum bridges

*A knowledge- or skills-bridge is a link between one area of the curriculum and another. For example, a case study on the devastating effects of an earthquake on a city in an economically less-developed country such as Haiti would include the knowledge-bridge of *economic inequality*. If you wish, you can guide pupils along this knowledge bridge and into the full content area of economic inequality and its effects on people, property and the environment.

Starters and plenaries are only part of the picture

We need to emphasise that although we think high quality starters and plenaries are essential to the best geographical learning, we recognise that they are not, of course, the *totality* of effective geography teaching. The bulk of every lesson you teach will focus on the main teaching and learning that will either lead on from the starter or take place before learning is brought to a conclusion in the plenary. This book focuses on starters and plenaries to draw attention to the crucial role they can play in creating successful geography pupils, despite the comparatively small amount of time they take up in lessons.

Get in touch

We would be very pleased to hear from you to find out how your pupils get on with the activities in this book, as well as your perspectives on the pros and cons of the starters and plenaries from a teacher's point of view. We would also be delighted if you could share any particularly successful starters/plenaries of your own making, together with details of why you feel they worked especially well. All such contributions will be acknowledged and considered for future editions of this book, or the companion website. You can contact us at: brinbest1967@gmail.com

How to use this book

We have tried to make this book as user-friendly as possible by including plenty of structure and sub-headings in the starters and plenaries, and by providing step-by-step guidance on how to use the entries in your classroom.

The book is made up of over 40 entries, each comprising a starter and a plenary linked together by a common theme. We have aimed for maximum flexibility by including starters and plenaries that, although linked through their topic, can be used as stand-alone activities as well as in tandem with each other. The activities start off by listing the main topic covered and the key geographical questions and with a short introduction about when to use the starter and plenary.

The majority of entries include pupil activities at three different levels:

E Easy
M Moderate
C Challenging.

The exact choice of activities for any teaching group, however, should be made according to the age and ability profile of the pupils in that group.

Further resources and stimulus materials to complement the text can be found in the companion website for this book which can be accessed at: www.bloomsbury.com/secondary-starters-and-plenaries-geography-9781441110916. This website also contains a comprehensive compendium of photographic images to be used in a variety of activities. Many of the pupil stimulus sections printed within this book can also be found on the website. A list of the online resources for the starter and plenary appears at the start of each new activity.

Section 1

Investigating geography

What is geography about?

Main topic: Defining the scope of geography as a subject.

Additional topic: The links between geography and other areas of study.

Key geographical questions:

- How can we describe the subject of geography to others?

- What links exist between geography and other subjects?

This starter and plenary are best used in the first couple of weeks of a new term, when pupils are making the transition from their previous years studying geography, reflecting on what has been learnt before and looking forward to new learning. It would also be interesting for pupils to repeat the tasks at the end of the school year, as this would show how their understanding of geography as a subject has changed as they have studied it further.

Starter

Pupil stimulus

To help your pupils connect with prior learning in geography start by drawing a collaborative mind-map of the topics they have studied before; taken together these subjects help make up the subject of geography. It is sensible to have ready several pre-prepared branches of the mind-map in case these are not suggested by your pupils – in particular the topics you feel are most central to the study of the subject.

Activities

❸ What is geography?

Ask the pupils to study the geography mind-map that you have prepared together, and think back to some of their favourite geography lessons. Ask them to imagine that they are trying to help pupils who are currently in Year 6 understand more about the subject of geography, and complete the following sentences:

- Geography is the study of…

- The most interesting parts of geography are…

- Geography is useful for life after school because…

Ⓜ The ideal geography pupil

In groups of four ask the pupils to look again at the geography mind-map you prepared together. Ask them to consider what the qualities of an *ideal geography pupil* would be. They should make a list of these qualities and then imagine they are giving advice to a Year 9 pupil making option choices. Ask them to write a paragraph aimed at these pupils under the title 'The personal qualities needed to succeed on a geography course'.

Ⓒ What is the value of geography?

Working with a learning partner, ask the pupils to discuss the value of geography in the 21st century. How can geography's place in the school curriculum be justified?

Teacher's tips

- As these tasks require pupils to express their personal opinions about geography, their responses are likely to be very varied. While many pupils will have wholly positive things to say about the subject, for others geography may be their least favourite lesson. Try not to take this too personally; at any point in time some pupils will be inspired more by other curriculum subjects, though some will come back to geography at a later stage (perhaps when the topics studied interest them more).

- It is important to allow all pupils to express their honest opinions when carrying out the above tasks, as this will help create the type of collaborative learning environment that engages pupils and results in greater success.

Plenary

Activities

Ⓔ Links to other subjects

Working with a learning partner, ask the pupils to write down three ways in which geography is linked to other subjects they have studied at school.

Ⓜ How does geography help?

Ask the pupils to imagine that they have to explain to their parents/guardians how their geographical studies have helped them with other subjects they have studied at school. Ask them to record what they would say.

ⓒ Subject links to geography

In a small group, ask the pupils to draw a simple table that shows which other school subjects are linked to geography (e.g. a tick-box type matrix with the different school subjects along the top row and geography in a column to the left).

Teacher's tip

If pupils are struggling to find connections between geography and other aspects of the curriculum you should provide some concrete examples. The most obvious links are probably with science (through topics such as earthquakes and the study/conservation of natural environments), maths (understanding and modelling physical and man-made processes) and history (understanding how places have come to be as they are today).

Extension

As an engaging extension of these activities, ask your pupils to prepare an entry for your school prospectus on the subject of geography. As prospectuses are written in a particular style it is important to let pupils study a real example before they begin the task. You may find that some of your pupils produce such high quality responses that you are able to use their work to promote the study of geography at your school. It is certainly very affecting and authentic to read about the subject in pupils' own words.

Can geography be a flavour?

Main topic: The effect of climate, soils and geology on crops.

Additional topic: The effect of global warming on the growth of fruit and vegetables in the UK.

Key geographical question: How does geography affect the growth and quality of fruit and vegetable crops?

Although these activities appear to be most suitable for use during a unit of work on agriculture, the unusual 'angle' of the Starbucks slogan means they can be slotted into any lesson as part of a fresh and thought-provoking learning episode.

Starter

Pupil stimulus

For many years the highly successful American-owned coffee-house chain Starbucks has used the thought-provoking advertising slogan 'Geography is a flavour'. This activity will get your pupils thinking about this slogan and what it means.

Activities
⒠ ⓜ ⒞ Thinking about the slogan

Explain to the pupils that they are going to let their classmates know what they think the Starbucks slogan means. They should think carefully about why this major coffee-house owner might say that 'Geography is a flavour' and how this slogan could portray the company positively. Ask them to write their ideas down ready to read out to the rest of the class. Ask each pupil in turn to read out their answers, while the others make notes. When you have heard all of the answers encourage the pupils to consider whether they want to change what they have written, or even write a new response.

Teacher's tip

If any pupils are struggling to understand the concept of geography being a flavour you should provide some additional targeted support to help them decode the slogan. For example, you could ask them the question, 'How could the geographical location of the coffee crop affect how the coffee plants grow and the taste of the coffee beans produced?'

Plenary

Pupil stimulus

The idea that products can taste differently according to the geographical location in which they grow is not new. The wine made from grapes that grew 2,000 years ago on the fertile slopes of Mount Vesuvius was renowned for its quality across much of Italy, before the notorious eruption of 79AD destroyed much of the surrounding area. In the activity below you will be asked to think about the landscapes, soils and climate of the UK and how these factors can affect food products such as fruit and vegetables and traditional British drinks such as apple juice, cider and beer.

Activities

🄴 Pick one

Ask the pupils to choose a specific fruit, vegetable or drink that is produced in the UK and name at least one way in which geography can affect how well it grows.

🄼 The best quality

For two fruits or vegetables (or drinks produced from them) produced in the UK, ask the pupils to identify the regions of Britain where the best quality fruit or vegetables grow.

🄶 New crops

Explain to pupils that global warming is set to expand the range of crops that can be grown in the UK. Ask the pupils to explain which new crops are likely to start growing here, where they will grow first and why this expansion is expected to occur.

Teacher's tips

- Bring some colour to the above lessons by bringing in examples of traditional British fruit and vegetables, and explaining their main growing requirements. You could also introduce pupils to some of the traditional ways of cooking or serving British fruit and vegetables – why not stage a testing session! (Do check for any food allergies first.)

- Some pupils may need to carry out some additional research in order to provide meaningful answers to the above tasks, and you could schedule some computer network time to allow them to do this.

Extension

Some British people are often surprisingly ignorant about the fruit and vegetable crops that grow in their country and the drinks which are made from these. A valuable extension activity would be to get your pupils to design a 'Did you know?'-type leaflet to help educate people about British-grown fruit and vegetables and the products they are made into.

Geographical news gathering by the general public

Main topic: The role of the general public in documenting geographical phenomena with their mobile phones/smartphones and tablet computers.

Additional topic: The regions of the world where news gathering by members of the public is often carried out.

Key geographical questions:

- How can the general public help document geographical news stories with their mobile phones/smartphones and tablet computers?

- Which parts of the world are especially fertile ground for geographical news gathering by members of the public?

These activities can be used very flexibly within a wide range of geographical learning and are ideal for spicing up a lesson or providing something different to help increase engagement.

Starter

Pupil stimulus

The general public is increasingly playing a part in documenting news stories of geographical interest, by taking photographs and video footage through cameras installed in their mobile phones/smartphones and tablet computers. The widespread availability today of these high-quality electronic devices has revolutionised news reporting, as it means that millions of people are out and about every day, equipped with the tools to be a news reporter. It has therefore become common to see dramatic images and video footage taken by the general public used in television news broadcasts and in national newspapers and their websites. Indeed, such material – taken by people who were 'on the spot' when the news story broke – sometimes now forms the centrepiece of news reporting, since it is often graphic, conveys a sense of what happened that words alone cannot do and provides a real immediacy. In this activity, ask the pupils to think about the type of geographical news events that can be most effectively documented by members of the public.

Activities

🅔 In the news

Ask the pupils to work with a learning partner and make a list of five news events of geographical interest that members of the public would be able to document especially well.

🅜 Likely and unlikely

Challenge the pupils to draw a two-columned table and in it list three news events of geographic interest that members of the public would be able to document especially well and three they would be *unlikely* to document well.

🅒 Is it a good idea?

Ask the pupils to consider the following question: Do you think it is good idea that the general public is able to contribute images and video footage of news events that are used by professional broadcasters and publishers? Ask them to record and justify their answer.

Teacher's tip

This topic will be brought alive if you are able to show your pupils some vivid examples of images and video taken by members of the public. The following case studies are particularly rich in imagery of this sort: the 2011 Japanese tsunami, any recent tornado strikes in the USA, the October 2013 St Jude storm in southern England.

Plenary

Pupil stimulus

In the following activity pupils will be asked to imagine they are involved in planning an overseas holiday for a group of geographical 'news chasers'. Rather like the 'storm chasers' who travel to the USA in search of incredible footage of tornadoes, news chasers are members of the general public with a passion for geography who want to have photographs or video footage they have taken published, for a wider audience to enjoy. They get a thrill from connecting with news stories and being the first person to take those all-important photographs or video frames.

Activities

❷ A good destination

Ask the pupils to choose a good destination for a news-chaser's holiday (state the country and location within that country) and explain why they have made this choice. Remember that they need to choose somewhere where geographically *newsworthy* events are likely to take place.

ⓜ Three locations

Ask the pupils to work with a learning partner and name three specific locations in the world that would be especially suitable destinations for a news-chaser's holiday.

❻ Sensitive locations

Working in groups of four, ask the pupils to discuss the following question: Are there any sensitive locations around the world that you would *not* want to send untrained news chasers too? They should explain their answer.

> ### Teacher's tip
>
> If your pupils are unfamiliar with specialist holidays of this nature, you could show them the websites/printed literature of some of the American storm-chasing companies, as this is probably the best-developed sector currently operating (there are also parallel companies offering to get you close to active volcanoes, glaciers etc.).

Extension

These activities would dovetail extremely well with the opportunity for your pupils to 'play reporter' in their own community. Although it is clearly not realistic to expect news events of national importance to regularly occur close to your school, pupils could use the video-capturing facilities of smartphones to conduct short interviews with members of the public on topics of geographical interest. The still/video cameras built into even basic sub-£100 phones yield impressive results and the material can be downloaded to a laptop or PC for permanent archival.

It is a good idea to purchase some low-cost smartphones for your department for these sort of activities if at all possible. Having a small bank of such smartphones for pupils to use also helps to avoid embarrassing pupils who do not their own device. Most smartphones can also be easily set up as dictaphones for camera-shy subjects, or for pupils to take verbal notes while 'in the field' – and of course the possibilities of using smartphone apps for geographical teaching are virtually endless and merit a book of their own.

Section 2

Geography through images

What's in a photograph?

Main topic: The use of photographs to explore geographical issues.

Additional topic: Bias in photographic evidence of places.

Key geographical questions:

• What can photographs tell us about the geographical world?

• How can bias distort what is shown in photographs?

Online resources: The online photograph bank.

These activities are extremely flexible and can be used at any time during a geography course. They challenge pupils to carefully analyse a variety of photographic images, and as they do so develop their analytical skills and ability to make accurate and relevant judgements as geographers about what they can see.

Starter

Pupil stimulus

A wealth of carefully-selected photographic images from around the world for your pupils to scrutinise can be found in the online resources that accompany this book. Each is labelled according to how it might be best used. The images represent the full spectrum of geographical topics, with each being thought-provoking, engaging or dramatic. They all encourage pupils to ask appropriate geographical questions about places, people or the environment. The images can be inserted into a PowerPoint presentation, or can be printed out on cards for pupils to study close-up.

Activities
❸ Looking at photographs

Explain to the pupils that they should choose one of the images provided and in a small group discuss the following questions:

• What can you see in the photograph? Make sure you look long and hard and really try to 'get into' the picture.

- Which topics have you studied in geography that could help you to understand what is happening in the photograph?

Ⓜ Features and conflicts

Explain to the pupils that they should choose one of the images provided and with a learning partner discuss the following questions:

- What are the main geographical features shown in the photos?

- Identify at least one *conflict* that is suggested in each photograph (for example, how are people conflicting with the environment? How are people conflicting with each other?).

- What further information would a geographer need to gather to help resolve the conflicts?

Ⓒ Location and features

Explain to the pupils that they should choose one of the images provided and in a small group discuss the following questions:

- Where in the world do you think this photograph taken? How accurate is it possible to be about the location of the image?

- What features of the photograph are most interesting to a geography pupil and why?

- Devise a series of questions that would help analyse what can be seen in the photograph.

Teacher's tips

- Photographic analysis can be a very powerful geographical tool, yet it is not systematically taught in many schools. Before letting your pupils loose on these tasks you should model the process of photo analysis with the group, so pupils understand the processes involved and how these can reveal meaningful geographical information.

- In particular, it is vital to encourage pupils to be really *observant* as they study photographs and to look beyond the superficial into the detail of the images. Some young people today tend not to be very observant in their day to day lives, so they may need to be re-trained in this regard!

Plenary

Pupil stimulus

For the following activities exploring *bias*, select the most interesting examples from the online photograph bank for your pupils to study. This bias, which could be motivated by a wide range of factors, could result from the photographer only capturing part of the scene, deliberately focusing on one aspect of the photograph or choosing to photograph something that is not representative of the place being captured. The key idea for the plenary is the possibility of bias in the photographs and the need to apply caution when interpreting what photographs appear to show.

Activities

🄴 Interesting features

Working in a group of four, ask the pupils to look carefully at the photograph provided. They should then answer the following questions:

- What are the most interesting things you can see in the photograph? Remember: do this with the eyes of a geography pupil!

- Who might disagree with something that is shown in the photograph? Why might they be unhappy about what they see?

🄼 What might be missing?

Ask the pupils to team up with two other people they don't usually work with, choose one of the photographs provided and study it closely. They should then answer the following questions:

- Why might the image not show the full picture of the place, people or environment shown?

- What extra details would need to be photographed to provide a fairer picture?

🄶 Is there any bias?

Ask the pupils to team up with a learning partner and look carefully together at one of the photographs provided. They should then answer the following questions:

- What sources of potential *bias* are there in the photograph?

- To what extent is it possible to be completely *objective* when taking photographs for geographical analysis?

Teacher's tips

- These plenary activities are among the most challenging in this book and most of your pupils are likely to need a fair amount of scaffolding to find them fully accessible. The key ideas that need to be understood are the concepts of *bias* and *objectivity* – both of which will require careful explanation and exemplification.

- Differentiation can be achieved by giving pupils carrying out the 'Easy' task just one specific photograph you have selected and providing those working on the 'Moderate' task with a choice of five suitable photographs. Pupils carrying out the 'Challenging' task can be given a free choice of photographs from the online photograph bank.

Extension

These activities, which it is envisaged will be carried out several times during the school year using different photographs, should enable your pupils to be much more sophisticated in future when they analyse photographs for geographical content. They should also be able to ask more appropriate geographical questions about specific places, people and environments.

This high level of photographic analysis may not be carried out in other departments in your school, so your pupils could prepare some useful posters for display around school, explaining the key steps in photographic analysis. These should emphasise the kind of information in photographs that is of most relevance to geographers and the type of questions that geography pupils ask to interpret and make sense of such images.

Googling the Amazon

Main topic: Place.

Additional topics: Space; interdependence; human processes; environmental action and sustainable development; cultural understanding and diversity.

Key geographical questions:

- What will the Google Street View project tell us about the geography of the Brazilian Amazon?

- What advantages and disadvantages will the Google Street View project bring to the Brazilian Amazon and to the UK?

Online resources: x2 photographs: Tumbira, north-west Brazil and Leeds, West Yorkshire, UK, both from Google Street View.

This starter and plenary can be used in any lesson which focuses on the people or habitats of the tropical rainforest, especially in South America. It is especially appropriate for the beginning of a teaching sequence about the tropical rainforest. It could also be used to explore the more general theme of interdependence between different countries, or the geographical implications for rich and poor countries of new technologies.

Starter

Pupil stimulus

The internet giant Google has recently launched an ambitious project to use its Street View technology to produce the first ever photographic record of the land-use and settlements on the banks of the upper Amazon river in north-west Brazil. The project team, using the same digital technology that was used to capture the Street View images of the UK which were launched in 2009, will take advantage of boats and a special tricycle to propel state-of-the-art camera equipment along rivers and dirt tracks. Google also plans to record images from *inside* selected buildings, allowing people to see what it is like to live and work in them.

The images collected will eventually be made available to every internet user across the world. Google is training local people to collect the images and the equipment will be left with them when the first survey is complete, allowing the work to continue into the future. The project is a collaboration between Google and the charity 'Foundation for a Sustainable

Amazon' (described in detail at www.google.co.uk/earth/outreach/stories/fas.html), which is keen to gather evidence that can be used to document the loss of the rainforest in this sensitive part of the Amazonian basin.

Activities

Download from the online resources the two photos that accompany this activity: 'The Amazon street view' and 'Leeds city centre'. Print them out and give them to the students, or display them on your whiteboard. They give an impression of what somebody viewing a Street View image of the two locations might see.

Working with a partner, ask the pupils to study the photographs carefully, then complete the following activities.

ⓔ Not in Leeds and not in the Amazon

Ask the pupils to list three things that the Street View camera is likely to capture in the Brazilian Amazon that would *not* be found in Leeds, UK. Next ask them to list three things that the Street View camera is likely to capture in Leeds, UK that would *not* be found in the Brazilian Amazon.

ⓜ In Leeds and the Amazon

Ask the pupils to list three things that the Street View camera is likely to capture in *both* the Brazilian Amazon and Leeds, UK.

ⓖ Relying on each other

Ask the pupils to identify one way in which the people living in the Brazilian Amazon and those living in Leeds, UK might be *interdependent* (i.e. rely on each other). For example, you might mention something they eat, something they make or something they do in their lives.

Teacher's tips

- Begin the lesson by locating north-west Brazil and Leeds, UK on a map. Show the pupils where the Amazon river begins and ends and the region the Google team will be working in (they will begin work in a town called Tumbira).

- Use the written part of the Pupil stimulus to prepare a verbal introduction to the topic, if this is preferred. Alternatively, pupils can be given the stimulus in written form. There are also some excellent reports on the internet about the Google Street View project in Brazil that might help you prepare for this lesson (e.g. http://news.cnet. com/8301-1023_3-57402062-93/google-brings-brazils-amazon-forest-to-street-view and www.bbc.co.uk/news/technology-14592184).

- Encourage pupils to develop their observation skills when looking at the images – e.g. by comparing and contrasting what they see; by looking for things at a variety of scales; by asking questions as they examine the images.

- Give pupils verbal-thinking prompts as they work through the questions – e.g. 'Can you see any kinds of vegetation?', 'How large are the houses and what are they made of?'; 'What can you see that is worth a lot of money?'; 'What kinds of animals might live in the places shown in the images?'.

- When the pupils have finished working through the questions, draw together the main points in a whole-class discussion. You could record some class answers to the 'Easy' and 'Moderate' tasks in a Venn diagram.

Plenary

Pupil stimulus

The Google Street View project is providing, for the first time, up-to-date images of land-use along key transport routes in a range of countries in the economically developed and less-developed world. This is giving people across the globe, who can view the internet, unprecedented access to geographical information about people, where they live and the impact they are having on the landscape. However, there are negative as well as positive aspects to the project, and not everyone agrees that it is a good idea for their homes and the surrounding area to be photographed for all to see.

Activities

The pupils should work in groups of about four to complete the following activities:

Ⓔ A positive development

Ask them to identify at least three reasons why people might feel the Google Street View project is a *positive* development in their locality. They should try to mention at least one reason that is relevant to Amazonian Brazil and a different one that is relevant to Leeds, UK. Encourage the pupils to consider things from the perspective of various different people (e.g. guest house owner; wildlife researcher; geography teacher).

Ⓜ A negative development

Ask the pupils to identify at least three reasons why people might feel the Google Street View project is a *negative* development in their locality. They should try to mention at least one reason that is relevant to Amazonian Brazil and a different one that is relevant to the Leeds, UK. Again, encourage them to consider things from the perspective of various people (e.g. a wealthy resident who owns two expensive cars; a farmer growing a banned crop; an indigenous Indian living in a remote tribe).

❻ What do you think?

On balance do the pupils feel that it is a good idea for Google to extend its Street View project to places such as Amazonian Brazil? Encourage them to express whether they strongly agree, agree, disagree or strongly disagree with this development? They should justify (give reasons for) their answer.

Teacher's tips

- More able pupils could be challenged to lead the group they are working in, or could not be shown the suggestions in brackets in the 'Moderate' activities. They could also be asked to complete the extension task below for homework, with no additional teacher support.

- Less able pupils could be arranged into a group which contains at least one more able pupil, or could be given one reason for the 'Moderate' activities to start them off, using one of the people mentioned in brackets. They could also be given some suggested headings for the 'Challenging' task (these will be given online).

- Encourage pupils to listen to the views of every member of their group before making any notes – this will be more likely if a leader is nominated to oversee the group's work.

- Gather the views of the groups in response to the 'Challenging' task and do not be reluctant at this stage to mention any important ideas that the pupils have missed – together with your own views.

- Make it clear to all pupils that there is no *right* answer to the 'Challenging' task – the important thing is that they are able to justify their views.

- Hold a vote to decide whether the class is in favour or against the expansion of Google Street View to Amazonian Brazil.

Extension

Ask the pupils to consider the following questions:

- How else is modern technology changing the way we can see the world?

- Why are these changes positive and why are they negative? Consider people, the economy and the environment.

Ask the pupils to write a 300-word article for a teen magazine on this topic, explaining their views to other young people their age.

'Interesting' geographical images

Main topic: Places and their geographical features.

Additional topic: Observing the world through photographs.

Key geographical questions:

- What do geographers see in photographs that is particularly interesting?

- Do some photographs provide more things of geographical interest than others?

Online resources: Series of photographs taken in different countries around the world.

Although these tasks could be carried out at any time, their synoptic nature and reliance on keen powers of observation make them more suitable as activities to use when pupils have covered a fair amount of geographical content, and when they are familiar with analysing photos.

Starter

Pupil stimulus

Download the series of photographs taken in different countries around the world which can be found in the online resources that accompany this book. Show them to your pupils and explain that they will be required to choose an image (or more than one image) that they think is particularly interesting from a geographical point of view.

Activities

⑤ Most interesting photo

Ask the pupils to select one of the photographs and give it a caption to explain why they think it is interesting from the point of view of a geography pupil. They should then share their work with a learning partner.

Ⓜ Label two photographs

Ask the pupils to select two of the photographs and add labels to both to show why, from a geographical perspective, they think they are interesting images.

Ⓒ Rank in order

Ask the pupils to study the photographs carefully and select three that, as a geography pupil, they find particularly interesting. Ask them to place them in rank order of how interesting they think they are and write a caption for each, justifying its rank.

Teacher's tips

- The concept of 'interesting' is obviously a rather subjective area for geography pupils, and as such you may find the responses to this activity to be quite varied – this is quite normal.

- It is important to let your pupils make autonomous choices as they search for interesting subjects in the images, and not to fall into the trap of thinking that they might only find stereotypical 'teenage' subjects such as shops, sports themes, 'cool' sites etc. interesting.

- Bear in mind that studying geography can be seen as the acquisition of knowledge and skills that enable pupils to think and talk like a professional geographer. Furthermore, the process by which pupils become proficient in these areas can be considered a *geographical apprenticeship*. With appropriate training, pupils should be able to put aside their personal interests as teenagers, wear their metaphorical geographer's hat and think like a professional. If they are able to do this successfully it will also give them a huge advantage in examination-type situations, which require pupils to enter into a quite different mode of thinking to their everyday world.

Plenary

Pupil stimulus

In this activity pupils will be asked to turn their attention to photographs they have taken themselves, during a holiday. They can either be images they have already printed out, or ones that are still in digital form on your smartphone, memory card etc.

Activities

❶ An interesting snap

Ask the pupils to find a photograph they took while on holiday that they think has considerable geographical interest. Ask them to label it to show why it is interesting and show it to two other members of the class.

ⓜ Captioning features

Ask the pupils to trawl through a range of photographs that they took while on holiday and identify three that show interesting geographical features. They should write a caption under each one explaining what can be seen and add their photographs to the display board in their classroom.

❻ Physical and human geography

Ask the pupils to have a good look over the most striking holiday photographs they have taken. Ask them to find two images that show features of special interest to a physical geographer and two of particular interest to a human geographer. They should then annotate each photograph to show its main features, then give it to you to put on the geography section of your school website.

Teacher's tips

- These activities will require some preparation as pupils need to have a suitable bank of holiday photographs to choose from in class. Pupils could select suitable images as a homework activity and bring these into class for labelling.

- It can be fun for pupils to select appropriate holiday snaps for the above activities with a parent/guardian or sibling. This gives them the enjoyment of 'revisiting' their holiday, while at the same time helping another person in their family to understand the subject of geography a little better (it is always advantageous for other family members to gain more insight into school subjects).

Extension

These activities should help to get geography pupils – and all those that see the holiday photographs – thinking like a geographer, both as they take photographs and as they analyse these at home. You can capitalise on this work by maintaining a permanent display board for holiday photographs (preferably in a prominent position in your school) and encouraging all pupils to add to this. You could even offer a termly prize for the best photograph (e.g. a geography-themed book or DVD). It is surprising how powerful this kind of measure can be in creating a culture in your school where geography is seen as subject that is both *interesting* and *relevant* to the day-to-day lives of pupils.

Looking for evidence of change

Main topic: Change in natural or man-made environments.

Additional topics: The effects of geographical change on people, property and the environment.

Key geographical question: How is our world changing as a result of natural or man-made processes?

Online resources: x3 photographs: One of place, one of landform and one of landscape.

These activities can be used at any point in a sequence of geography lessons, and have links with many different geographical topics.

Starter

Pupil stimulus

Change – of all types and at all scales – is an important theme in geography. As a consequence, it is often the subject of studies by professional geographers and these studies have an important influence on decision makers. To help them think about the topic of change, show your pupils the photographs from the online resources that go with this activity: one of place, one of landform and one of landscape. Their job is to look for evidence of change in this photograph.

Activities

ⓔ Changes in the future

Ask the pupils to identify three things in the photograph that are likely to change in the future.

ⓜ Natural and man-made changes

Ask the pupils to identify two things in the photograph that are likely to change *naturally* in the future and two things that are likely to be changed by the *actions of people*.

❻ Wealth of the country

Ask the pupils to what extent is it possible to determine the wealth of the country the photograph was taken in, judging from the changes they are provoked to think about when studying the image.

Teacher's tip

As with all activities involving the study of photographs, the above activities will require pupils to use their *close observation skills* in order to come up with appropriate responses. As such, it is vital to encourage your pupils to look – *then look again* in even greater detail – at the photograph to see the details that matter. If pupils are struggling to identify aspects of the photograph likely to change, you could help them with the following prompts:

• How might the natural features shown in the photograph change due to erosion/weathering/deposition/global process such as climate change?

• How could the buildings shown in the photograph get more dilapidated/bigger/more professionally built?

• How could the livelihoods/job prospects of people living where the photograph was taken decline/improve?

• How might quality of life for people living where the photograph was taken improve/get worse?

• How could the environment shown in the photograph be improved/made worse by people?

• How could any problems shown in the photograph be tackled and what would the result be?

Plenary

Pupil stimulus

This activity asks pupils to imagine they are a photographer whose job it is to take images of their home settlement that show that it is *changing*. They will be asked to think about the settlement in which they live (or the one closest to your home) and identify locations where change is taking place.

Activities

🄴 The best location

Ask the pupils to consider where would the best location be in their settlement to take a photograph that would illustrate that change of some kind is taking place? They should explain why this is the best location.

🄼 Different kinds of changes

Ask the pupils to identify three locations in their settlement where they could take photographs that would show that change of *different* kinds is taking place?

🄲 Poster

Working in a small group, ask the pupils to carry out a thought-shower exercise to identify the images that they would need to take to illustrate a poster on the theme of change in their settlement.

Teacher's tips

- Help stimulate your pupils' thinking by showing them images taken in settlements outside their home region that illustrate change.

- Photographers work at a variety of scales and your pupils may want to think about what wide-angle, landscape-type shots might show compared to close-up, detailed images of human life or the natural world.

Extension

Ask the pupils to go out into their home settlement to take photographs of the locations that best demonstrate change. These could be combined to make a large annotated poster for display in your school, or could be posted on your school website as part of a geography department feature on change in the local area.

Images that convey geographical meaning

Main topic: The use of images to represent countries and smaller regions.

Additional topic: How people's views on their home region varies.

Key geographical questions:

- How can images convey **geographical** *meaning* about countries and smaller geographical areas?

- How do the choices of people regarding the images chosen to represent their home area vary?

These activities can be used very flexibly within your geography lessons, though better outcomes will be achieved if pupils tackle them after they have had the chance to reflect on the distinctive geographical features of their home country and region.

Starter

Pupil stimulus

This activity requires pupils to think about the images that sum up the geography of the country in which they live. Note that they will not be choosing *actual photographs*; instead they will be *imagining* the images that would show the geography of their country particularly well. These could feature natural or man-made subjects or a combination of both.

Activities

❸ Distinctive features

Ask the pupils to think about the distinctive geographical features of their country and identify up to five 'images' that would sum up these features. They should then swap their ideas with a learning partner and make a note of the number of images they have chosen that are similar, or even the same.

Ⓜ Physical features

Ask the pupils to select between five and ten 'images' to go into a book that presents the main *physical* features of their country. Then, working in a small group, they should justify their selections and listen carefully to those of the others in their group.

Ⓒ Physical and human geography

Working with a learning partner, ask the pupils to make a list of the ten 'images' that best represent the physical geography of their country and another ten that best portray the human geography of their country.

Teacher's tips

- Encourage your pupils to look over their notes on all the main curriculum topics to help them get the best possible representation of geographical content in their 'images'.

- Show your pupils extracts from travel brochures to give examples of how visually-strong images are used to convey the feel of a place.

Plenary

Pupil stimulus

Explain to the pupils that they will now move on to think about their country at a finer scale by concentrating on the county or region in which they live. Once again, they will be thinking about images that portray a sense of what their home county or region is like, this time with a view to creating a visual 'emblem' that is representative of the area and could go on the county/regional logo or crest.

Activities

Ⓔ Create an emblem

Ask the pupils to devise an emblem for their home county or region by choosing the *single image* that they think best portrays its character. Their emblem could be a person, animal, plant, natural feature (e.g. mountain, valley, river, lake etc.), building, monument or something else entirely – the choice is yours. Tell them to be prepared to explain why they have chosen their image when they are asked.

Ⓜ Letter to the editor

Ask the pupils to write an imaginary letter to the editor of your regional newspaper suggesting the image that should go on your county/regional logo or crest. Ask them to use *persuasive* language to explain their opinion.

Ⓖ Representing viewpoints

Ask the pupils to identify the image that *best* represents their home county or region and could go on a logo/crest for it. They should then identify additional images that the following two people might choose: a) Somebody who is *optimistic* about the area; b) Somebody who is *pessimistic* about the area.

Teacher's tips

- You should remind pupils that this is a *creative* exercise and there are no 'correct' answers as such – instead the challenge is for pupils to use their creativity to think of an image that they feel fits the character of their county or region especially well.

- Pupils would benefit from seeing a range of national and county-level emblems, logos or crests from different countries around the world to help them see how images are used in this context.

Extension

These activities could lead on to the creation of a stunning photo-montage showing the geographical features of your pupils' home country or county/region. This is an endeavour that pupils and staff outside the geography department (and indeed people in the wider community) could get involved in, as everybody is likely to have a view on the images that best sum up their country or county/region.

It could also stimulate some interesting work to devise a crest for your school that incorporates geographical themes, which geography pupils take a lead in organising.

The whole picture?

Main topic: Photographic analysis.

Additional topic: Bias in photographic images.

Key geographical questions:

- In what ways may photographs not give you the whole picture of a location?

- How can photographs of places be made more representative?

Online resources: Choose a photograph from the online photograph bank that only shows part of the 'whole picture' of something.

These are very flexible activities that can be used at many alternative points during a geography course. They do, however, require pupils to be familiar with looking carefully at photographs, so should be attempted only after some work to develop this skill has been carried out.

Starter

Pupil stimulus

Select a photograph from the photograph bank in the online resources that, for various reasons, only shows part of the 'whole picture' of a location.

Activities

ⒺWhat's missing?

Working with a learning partner, ask the pupils to study the photograph you have given to them. Ask them to consider why it might not show the whole picture of the place featured. What is missing in the photograph?

ⓂThe 'whole picture'

In a small group, ask the pupils to study the photograph you have given to them and identify one additional *physical* feature and one additional *human* feature that they would need to capture to ensure it better presents a sense of the 'whole picture' of the place in the photograph.

⑥ A balanced picture

Ask the pupils to imagine they have been given the task of producing a *balanced* picture of the location featured. What additional things would they need to include in the photograph to make it more representative of the place featured?

Teacher's tips

- Several of the photographs in the accompanying online photograph bank would be suitable for this activity, though the final choice is yours.

- It is important that pupils do not take the concept of the 'whole picture' too literally. Clearly, no photograph can show the totality of a place, and this activity asks pupils to embrace the metaphorical sense of 'whole picture'.

- Pupils may find it helpful if you ask them to imagine that the photograph can go 'wide-angle', so they can see what is situated to the left and right of a central image.

- Provide hints to help pupils appreciate the various ways in which images may not show the whole picture, as follows: could the missing features be larger/smaller, newer/older, richer/poorer, cleaner/dirtier etc.

Plenary

Pupil stimulus

This activity will get the pupils thinking about taking their own photographs that show the 'whole picture' of their home settlement, or another one they know well.

Activities
⑥ Representing your settlement

Ask the pupils to identify a location for a photograph within their chosen settlement that would show you the 'whole picture' of the settlement well. They should then choose a different location that would *not* represent their settlement very well.

⑳ Choosing three locations

If the pupils were only able to use three photographs to convey the 'whole picture' of their chosen settlement, where would they take these images? Ask them to explain why these locations are particularly suitable.

❻ Create a table

Ask the pupils to draw a two-columned table and label the columns 'Representative location' and 'Non-representative location'. They should think about their chosen settlement and for each column in the table add the names of at least five photographic locations within the settlement that illustrate the concept of representative or non-representative locations particularly well.

Teacher's tip

Pupils may find it helpful to begin this activity by undertaking an imaginary walk through their chosen settlement, to remind them of some of its main features. This would also be a convenient time to ask them: How well do they know the back streets and hidden areas of the settlement? If they have only shaky knowledge of these areas you should help to fill in the gaps, because this lack of knowledge could prevent them from making accurate judgements.

Extension

These activities could be drawn together by asking pupils to prepare an A4 poster containing a bullet-point list of advice on how to ensure that photographs of locations are representative and show a good sense of the 'whole picture' of the place. There are links here with the use of photographic (and artistic) images in history as sources of *evidence*, which you may want to exploit in collaboration with the history department.

Section 3

Managing urban areas

Looking at cityscapes

Main topic: Place.

Additional topics: Physical and human processes; space; visual literacy.

Key geographical questions:

- What can photographs of the London cityscape tell us about the geography of the city?

- In what other ways are photographs a useful tool for geographers?

Online resources: x2 photographs: the view from the London Eye looking north-west and the view from the London Eye looking north-east.

This activity is primarily designed to help pupils develop their observation skills. Close observation and interpretation of photographs is an important geographical skill that is often neglected in schools. The activity would provide an ideal introduction to most topics related to the geography of urban areas.

Starter

Pupil stimulus

Show the pupils the two online photographs that accompany this starter, both taken from the London Eye, one showing the view looking north-west and the other looking north-east. Ask them to look closely at the London cityscape photographs, then work through the following tasks.

Activities
🅔 🅜 Labelling features

Provide the pupils with copies of the photographs and ask them to label the following things:

- the river Thames

- Big Ben and the Houses of Parliament

- three other tourist attractions

- a place where a wealthy person might live

- an area of low environmental quality.

⦿ Comparing cityscapes

Ask the pupils to think about the city closest to where they live. They should imagine they are looking at a photograph of its cityscape. What would it have in common with the London cityscape and what would be different?

Teacher's tips

- Make sure pupils are familiar with the position of London within southern England and with key landmarks such as the river Thames.

- Some facts about the London Eye should help to engage pupils' interest. For example, it is the world's highest cantilevered observation wheel, rising to 135 metres above the ground. Ask any pupils who have been on the wheel to tell the rest of the class what it was like.

- As an extra challenge, more able pupils could label an additional five features of interest on each photograph.

Plenary

Pupil stimulus

Ask the pupils to imagine that they are going to set up a website to show people the good and bad features of their village, town or city. The website will include videos, photographs and text.

Activities

⦿ Choosing locations

Ask the pupils to identify five locations in their settlement where they would take photographs for the website. They should explain why they have chosen these specific locations.

Teacher's tips

- To help your pupils identify suitable locations, encourage them to take an 'imaginary tour' in their head around their settlement, during which they visit the good and bad parts.

- Estate agent descriptions of settlements (on house sale information sheets, now widely available online) are good places to look for positive descriptions of what they have to offer.

- More able pupils can be challenged to identify eight to ten locations for photography in their settlement.

Extension

Several famous photographers have recorded the cityscapes of the world's major cities in striking and dramatic images that are now on display in art galleries or museums. Using their research skills ask the pupils to find out about the work of one of these photographers (good examples of such work can be found at http://andrewprokos.com, http://jeffovers.co.uk and www.willbartonphotography.com). What does their work tell us about one city they have photographed?

The value of sustainable urban drainage systems (SuDS)

Main topic: Management of the built environment in response to the onset of climate change.

Key geographical questions:

- Why is the control of surface water in towns such an important issue?

- What are the methods of control? How can we all benefit?

Online resources: Printable pupil stimulus materials; SuDs information sheet.

These tasks will usefully contribute to a discussion about the impact of global warming on the environment. Pupils will be able to focus on current imaginative initiatives being rolled out to manage surface water in towns. The key to the success of these schemes is that the flow of the water is slowed down.

Starter

Pupil stimulus

Sustainable urban drainage systems (SuDS)

SuDS are systems that are built into the urban environment with the aim of improving the management of rain and surface water by slowing down its journey to the river.

Slow is good
Open ground, such as fields and gardens, soaks up rainwater and slows down its journey. Water seeps into the ground where it moistens the soil and so nourishes the plants. The soil then filters the water before it slowly enters the river system. The water system of an area is complex and the components need to be in balance if it is to work properly.

The problem of fast run-off
When rain falls into a city it falls on to hard surfaces – the roofs of the buildings, the

pavements, the roads and so forth. From here it runs into the gutters and then into the sewers before very quickly pouring into the nearby river. Many gardens have been paved over and this hard surface also increases the run-off into the drainage system. The fast-moving water takes the pollutants from the streets straight into the rivers where they can damage the water quality and the natural habitats and the animals and plants that depend on them downstream. The water rapidly flows into the rivers causes them to fill quickly and flood, often with tragic results.

SuDS are designed to slow down the flow of water so that it is nearer to its natural speed.

Advantages of SuDS

Reduced risk of flooding
Water runs through the system in a more manageable way and flooding is avoided.

Reduced risk of pollution
The slower movement of water enables the soil to act as a natural filter of pollutants.

Benefits for people
SuDS enhance the look of an urban area and its amenity value – plants and gardens take the place of paved areas.

Benefits for wildlife
SuDS create urban habitats for wildlife and have a positive diversifying effect on those habitats downstream.

Provide the pupils with a copy of the 'SuDS information sheet' (available from the online resources for this book) to see what a SuDS looks like, before asking them to complete the tasks below.

Activities

E Paving the garden

Many people have turned their front gardens into paved areas for their cars. Ask the pupils to discuss with your learning partner the pros and cons of doing this. Ask them to make a chart with two columns, 'Pros' and 'Cons', and see which has the most thoughts in it after five minutes.

M Amenity value

One of the features of SuDS is their 'amenity value', that is how good they are for the people living in the area. Ask the pupils to consider what they think is the value of such things as water gardens and ponds in public places? Are there any drawbacks?

⊙ Educational value

Ask the pupils to examine the school case study on the 'SuDS information sheet'. Ask them to discuss with a learning partner what exactly the educational value of an artificial wetland might be on or near the school playground. They should make a note of their thoughts to share with other pairs. Do they think there could be any problems that would need to be addressed? Ask them to make a note of these.

Teacher's tips

- Working in pairs is the better way to approach these tasks. The material online and the suggested links provide some vivid pictures for the pupils to work on.

- A very comprehensive document on sustainable drainage systems is published jointly by the RSPB and the Wildfowl and Wetlands Trust (WWT) and is available at: http://www.rspb.org.uk/Images/SuDS_report_final_tcm9-338064.pdf

- At http://www.susdrain.org/case-studies/ there are brief reports of SuDS case studies from across the country. These are useful because they show the small scale of many of the projects making them accessible to the pupils. There is also the possibility of there being a project near you that can be referred to directly.

Plenary

Pupil stimulus

Green roofs and living walls

On the 'SuDS information sheet' online there are links to images of green roofs and living walls. Ask the pupils to look carefully and critically at these images. They are systems and like all systems they depend on several components working together. Ask them to make a note of the features that strike them as being interesting or important and then complete the tasks below.

Activities

⊕ Green roofs

Ask the pupils to discuss and note down the features that they see in the pictures of the green roofs (including the goats on the roof) – what are the value of these?

Ⓜ Living walls

Ask the pupils to discuss and note the advantages and disadvantages of living walls. They should think of the practical considerations, the ecological value and the aesthetic value of these features of modern architecture.

Ⓒ Green buildings

Ask the pupils to look at the images of living walls and green roofs online and the photograph and the diagram on the 'SuDS information sheet' (online). To what extent do they feel that isolated buildings like this provide little overall benefit and what we need is a great many such buildings if any impact is going to be made?

Extension

Pose the question: Should we be farming in the sky? Show the pupils the images in this link:

http://www.treehugger.com/sustainable-product-design/sky-farm-proposed-for-downtown-toronto.html

Ask them to consider whether this is the future of farming for food in an urban environment?

Improving Sheffield city centre

Main topic: Urban regeneration.

Additional topic: Improving the quality of life in an urban setting.

Key geographical questions:

• What have the authorities done to improve Sheffield city centre over the last ten years?

• What positive effects has this had on the city centre?

Online resources: Improving city centre PowerPoint presentation; Regeneration measures flash cards.

This is an ideal entry to use either at the start or at the end of a unit of work on urban areas. It encourages pupils to think about the various ways in which city centres can be regenerated, using one of the best examples of city centre renaissance in the UK.

Starter

Pupil stimulus

A PowerPoint presentation can be found in the online resources which provides information about city centre improvements in Sheffield – England's fourth largest city, including details on the Supertram network. the Winter Garden, Tudor square and the rail station frontage. Pupils should also be given a copy of flashcards (see also the online resources) that depict the ten regeneration measures shown in the PowerPoint presentation. Also provide them with the information 'The views of a local resident' below, before asking them to complete the activities.

The views of a local resident

'One of my favourite parts of Sheffield city centre is the area around the Peace Garden. The authorities have spent a lot of money landscaping this area and planting many trees and flowers, and you can even see wildlife there. There are always lots of people enjoying themselves in the Peace Garden; in summer children head to this part of this city to play in the special fountains that shoot up from the pavement and often soak them! One of the great things about the regeneration of the city is that people are really using the new facilities we have in Sheffield. The Winter Garden, which was opened by the Queen in 2003, is the largest urban glasshouse in Europe, and attracts over two million visitors a year. You always see people reading, chatting, relaxing or playing with their children in there. I think we should be really proud of what we have here in the city of Sheffield.'

Caroline Essery

Activities

🅴 Considering the improvements

Working in groups of three or four, ask the pupils to sort the Sheffield flashcards into two piles as follows:

1 Improvements designed chiefly to encourage more shoppers to visit the city

2 Improvements designed chiefly to improve environmental quality in the city

Ask them if there any measures that belong equally in both piles? They should then share their work with another group and discuss any differences in their answers.

🅼 How important are the improvements?

Ask the pupils to work with a learning partner to arrange the Sheffield flashcards in order of the importance of each project in regenerating the city centre. To show this they could lay them out in a line, or in another suitable pattern (e.g. a diamond or triangular arrangement). Tell them to be ready to justify their views to the rest of the class.

🅲 Choosing a focus

Ask the pupils to imagine they are going to give a talk on the success of urban regeneration in Sheffield to city planners from around Europe. If they had to focus on just *three* of the projects on the flashcards what would they be and why?

Teacher's tips

- Before beginning work on this topic, it is important to assess how familiar your pupils are with urban areas and the methods used to regenerate them. If your school is situated in a mainly rural area, or in a region supporting only towns and villages, you will need to make sure that you do some background work to establish a basic knowledge-base and to ensure that your pupils are familiar with the essential vocabulary of urban areas.

- Google StreetView is an excellent means of analysing some of the principal features of urban areas, and could also be used by your pupils to explore specific aspects of Sheffield city centre.

Plenary

Pupil stimulus

You should aim to provide a suitable stimulus linked to the city or town closest to the pupils' school. The activities encourage pupils to think about the measures that would improve their local settlement, including those mentioned in the Sheffield case study.

Activities

❸ Improving your local town or city

Ask the pupils to consider the positive and negative features of their local city or town. Ask them to identify three things that could be done to improve the centre of the settlement and explain how it would be better for people because of their improvements.

❿ Would they work?

Ask the pupils to look back to their work on Sheffield. Of all the regeneration measures that have been tried in that city which ones stand the best chance of working in their local settlement? They should draw a horizontal line with the label 'Suitable for my local settlement' at one end and 'Not suitable for my local settlement' at the other. Then they should write each regeneration measure along the line in the place they feel it belongs.

❻ In the news

Ask the pupils to write a short newspaper article describing how the centre of their local city or town could be improved for the benefit of people and the environment.

Teacher's tip

- Those pupils whose local settlement *is* Sheffield should select a different city or town for the tasks in the plenary – for example a settlement near to one of their relations.

- You should try to get your pupils to be creative and think of novel regeneration strategies for their local settlement, which are relevant to the challenges it is currently facing.

Extension

The concept of *regeneration* is an important one within geography, that can be applied to a variety of contexts. Although usually referring to processes that occur in urban areas, it is also possible to see regeneration at work in rural settings. Ask your pupils to consider the various ways in which regeneration is improving the quality of life in their home county for all sections of the community. This is a productive research exercise, and pupils should be directed to the websites of their local council/development agency, which are likely to include details of the key projects that have taken place.

Managing visitors to York

Main topic: Managing the damaging effects of tourism.

Additional topic: The challenge of managing the urban environment.

Key geographical questions:

- How can visitors be managed at sites with high numbers of tourists?

- How can the value of sites be maintained while at the same time meeting the needs of their visitors?

Online resources: Printable pupil stimulus material; photographs taken in York city centre.

This is an ideal series of tasks to carry out after your pupils have studied the generic issues around the challenge of managing cities in the 21st century. In particular, they should have at least some understanding of the main methods that have been used by city managers to deal with the high numbers of visitors in cities. There are links between the activities in this entry and those in the starter and plenary entitled 'What's in a photograph?' (see page 15) which deals with photo analysis. Pupils will be better equipped to work through the tasks in this entry if they have had some prior experience of analysing photographs.

Starter

Pupil stimulus

Provide the pupils with the information about York, below, as well as the collection of photographs from the online resources that have been taken in York city centre. before asking them to complete the activities.

Hundreds of years of living history

York is one of Britain's great cities, with a reputation that goes far beyond the four counties of Yorkshire that bear its name. As well as being an important commercial and residential centre (it had 153,000 inhabitants in 2011), this northern English city is famous for its magnificent 600-year-old cathedral, York Minster, as well as its well-preserved boundary walls and its unusual Medieval street layout, which is still lined with numerous historic buildings. York's many internationally-renowned museums include the JORVIK

Viking Centre, which is home to a reconstruction of a 1,000-year-old Viking settlement that was found beneath the modern city of York, and was the subject of a famous archaeological excavation in the 1970s.

Every year, millions of tourists visit the city of York; these visitors include large numbers of UK-based tourists, together with huge numbers of visitors from across Europe, the USA, Japan and many other countries. During their visits, these tourists rub shoulders along busy streets with the residents that call York home, together with the tens of thousands of people that commute to the city every day to work. Banking, legal and property services are just three of the economic activities that take place in York city centre – in addition, of course, to the many tourist-related businesses.

The city authorities in York have put in place various measures to manage all the visitors to their great city, many of whom often have conflicting interests. This work has been driven by the need to find practical solutions to the challenges presented by high visitor numbers, while at the same time ensuring that the historic and cultural value of the city is not damaged. The authorities must also bear in mind that York is a working city with thousands of shops, services and other businesses that provide employment and help to boost the prosperity of the city and the wider region.

Photographs are an excellent way to consider some of the key issues in York today. Look at the variety of online images taken in the city that illustrate important locations that need to be managed. They demonstrate the distinctive character of York and show how land-use varies across the city.

Activities

🄴 Managing tourists

Ask the pupils to choose three images of York and identify five ways in which the York city authorities have tried to manage tourists.

🄼 Tourist flashpoints

Ask the pupils to study the York photographs and find three potential *tourist flashpoints* where visitors need to be managed especially carefully. They should explain why each could be a flashpoint and suggest what measures the city authorities could introduce to manage the problems that might occur there.

🄲 Presentation to planners

Ask the pupils to look over all the photographs of York and imagine they are going to be making a short presentation to an audience of urban planners about how visitors to the city are being managed. They should identify the main headings for the presentation, making sure they mention the full range of methods shown in the photographs.

Teacher's tips

- This case study could be illuminated with video footage of York, of which there is much excellent material available via www.youtube.com (see the online resources for specific web-links).

- Encourage your pupils to make their own novel suggestions for how visitors in York could be managed, as well as spotting examples of actual measures that have already been attempted. You should explain that city decision-makers in many cities in the UK are still struggling to manage people, and those in York have yet to exhaust all the possibilities!

- The JORVIK Viking Centre website has some excellent material that makes tangible the long history of settlement in the area now occupied by York – including analysis of ancient human excrement to show what the residents of the settlement ate! (http://jorvik-viking-centre.co.uk).

Plenary

Pupil stimulus

Managing the effects of tourism is becoming an increasingly difficult challenge in many parts of the UK and overseas, as more people use their leisure time and hard-earned income to explore places of interest – both within cities and in more rural areas. The pupils should consider how visitors to a tourist site that they know well have been managed (either at a site near home or one further afield – it could be in the UK or overseas), then answer one of the questions below.

Activities

ⓔ Management issues

Ask the pupils to identify three of the management issues at the chosen tourist site that are similar to those in York and two issues that are different.

ⓜ Lessons to learn

Ask the pupils to consider what the authorities that are managing the chosen tourist site could learn from how visitors have been managed in York? They should give examples to explain their answer.

⊙ Cartoon

Ask the pupils to devise a short 'stick-person' cartoon strip that would explain to overseas visitors, who do not speak English very well, what they need to do to reduce their impact on the tourist site you have chosen.

Teacher's tips

- The type of tourist sites selected by your pupils could be extremely varied and may be quite different to the York example. To help provide an overview of the selected sites it would be sensible to share their choices with other members of the class.

- The pupils tackling the 'Challenging' task should be given the opportunity to study examples of 'stick-person' cartoons and how these are used to convey important messages to visitors.

Extension

These activities lead on to the wider issue of whether there is a threshold above which visitor numbers to a site or attraction are simply not sustainable.

A meaningful follow-up research exercise would involve pupils identifying locations where more draconian management actions have been necessary – in particular the restriction of visitor numbers or even the closing of certain sites. The Lascaux caves in south-western France, with their incredible ancient animal paintings, are a particularly powerful example to consider. These caves, now a UNESCO World Heritage Site, have been have been closed to tourists to protect the internationally-important artwork, which was painted on the cave walls about 17,000 years ago (see http://www.lascaux.culture.fr/?lng=en#/fr/00.xml for an amazing 3D tour of the caves). The pros and cons of restricting visitor numbers to such sites can be considered, as well as the ethics of completely closing some sites to visitors.

Retail heaven in Leeds?

Main topic: Retail developments in cities.

Additional topic: The urban economy.

Key geographical questions:

- What benefits can a major retail development bring to a city?

- Do major retail developments have any drawbacks for those who work and live in cities?

Online resources: Printable pupil stimulus material; a series of photographs and videos taken in Trinity Leeds.

These are ideal activities for pupils to carry out before they start a unit of work on the retail sector or urban development. Both the starter and plenary deal with some of the most significant issues affecting cities in economically developed countries today, as different economic sectors jostle to become dominant.

Starter

Pupil stimulus

Provide pupils with the following information as well as the series of photographs and videos about taken in Trinity Leeds, before asking them to complete the activities.

Flagship Leeds shopping centre opens its doors

The £350 million Trinity Leeds shopping centre, which finally opened in March 2013 after several years of construction, was one of the most significant retail building projects to take place within a British city for decades. It was also the only new shopping centre to open in the UK during the whole of 2013. The centre aims to offer the highest quality shopping experience ever achieved in the UK, with a number of unique or highly distinctive features, including:

- Over 100 shops, bars and restaurants, including an excellent mix of *prestige-brand* shops such as a major Apple shop alongside more familiar high-street names such as Next and Boots. The total space dedicated to shops and services in the centre is one million square feet.

- A *customer service lounge* equipped with tables and chairs where visitors can relax, chat and have a pit-stop. The centre also offers free drinks, a library equipped with Leeds-themed books and newspapers, free-to-use iPads and an information service.

- *Numerous restaurants* and *'Trinity Kitchen'*, a dedicated food and drink area with various high-quality cafés and bars, plus vendors selling award-winning street food. The aim has been to provide tasty food in the centre for people on a wide variety of budgets – from students and families wanting a great value bite to eat, to those with more money to spend, who are seeking a fine-dining experience.

- *Customer advisers* patrolling the centre with iPads to give advice to customers and conduct surveys.

- *Free Wi-Fi* throughout the centre, which is bringing in lots of young people who take advantage of this service to surf the net and download apps without incurring network charges.

- A *specially-designed mobile and tablet app* for the centre, giving information on the shops and services you will find there, announcements of special offers and details of one-off events.

- Many *comfortable seating areas* for socialising, relaxing and planning your shopping strategy.

- A *high-quality cinema* showing the latest movie releases as well as old classics. To improve the visitor experience, adult movie-goers are allowed to take their own wine into the auditorium, which they consume while watching the film from the comfort of plush sofas.

- What have been described as *'the best public toilets in Leeds'*, offering gents, ladies and disabled toilets plus dedicated baby-changing facilities, all of which are kept scrupulously clean by dedicated staff.

- High-quality *artistic sculptures* within the centre, including a huge packhorse crafted out of galvanised steel by the internationally-renowned Scottish sculptor Andy Scott.

- Regular *special events* such as theatrical performances, dance shows and concerts, all held under the dramatic glass roof of the centre.

An impressive 12 million people visited the centre in the first seven months after it opened.

Activities

Ask the pupils to work in a small group to study these visual stimuli and complete the tasks.

ⓔ Benefits to the city of Leeds

Ask the pupils to make a list of the benefits that Trinity Leeds is likely to bring to the city.

ⓜ Pros and cons

Ask the pupils to list five benefits of Trinity Leeds that the city council will be pleased to see. Then they should list three negative aspects of the development which could affect other groups or individuals in Leeds.

ⓒ Success criteria

Ask the pupils to imagine they are reviewing the success of Trinity Leeds three years after it opened. They should decide which criteria they would use to judge how successful it has been, then list them in order of importance (giving justification for each).

Teacher's tip

Most teenagers are pretty savvy about shopping and the relative merits of different brands – indeed a fair proportion of young people consider shopping to be one of their main 'hobbies'. As such, most of your pupils should be able to make their own judgements about Trinity Leeds from the list of shops provided online.

Plenary

Pupil stimulus

Over the last few years in the UK, several high-profile shops have disappeared from the high street. These include the electrical goods retailer Comet and the clothing store Peacocks – with other big names such as the camera-specialist Jessops and the music store HMV only just being saved. These bankruptcies have caused concern to city planners and local/central government, who all believe that thriving city centres are essential to the economic success of modern Britain.

Activities

ⓔ Shops and services

Ask the pupils to think about why is it important that city centres in the UK continue to have a wide range of shops and services?

ⓜ Make your point

Ask the pupils to write a paragraph for each of the following, explaining why they would want British cities to have thriving central areas, with many different shops and services: the Chamber of Trade Association; The Union of Shopworkers; The Consumer Association Which?

ⓒ The national economy

Ask the pupils to consider: How can successful city centres help boost the national economy of the UK?

Teacher's tip

You may have to explain to your pupils the role of the three organisations listed in the 'Moderate' task, plus the issues that interest them.

Extension

These activities would be an excellent prelude to a more in-depth study by your pupils of a shopping centre of their choice. Groups of pupils could team-up to produce a simple website, factsheet or poster about their chosen shopping centre, highlighting its main features and the benefits it has brought with it. The managers of such centres are usually very accommodating when it comes to sending pupils appropriate background literature, and some will even offer a guided tour.

Section 4
Managing rural areas

Connecting rural communities sustainably

Main topic: Sustainable transport.

Additional topics: Environmental action, sustainable development and place.

Key geographical questions:

- In a rural and protected environment such as the Yorkshire Dales, how can visitors and local communities be encouraged to take more sustainable journeys?

- How might the promotion of safe journeys for pedestrians and cyclists help the image of the Yorkshire Dales National Park as a nationally protected area?

Online resources: The Yorkshire Dales National Park Authority press release.

These activities would work well as an introduction to geographical issues in a national park, as they get pupils thinking about the landscape and human features of such an area. They allow pupils to explore a range of issues, including the management of tourism (especially traffic congestion) and how community priorities within a national park can be maintained.

Starter

Pupil stimulus

The activities in this entry centre on a project, organised by the Yorkshire Dales National Park Authority, to encourage people to use electric bicycles as a sustainable form of transport. The aim of the project was to develop a network of locations where electric bicycles could be hired (e.g. bed and breakfast establishments), together with a series of battery-charge points. The hope was that the project would act as a sustainable tourism initiative which would encourage more local spending by visitors to the Yorkshire Dales. Show the pupils the press release that can be found online, which was sent out to assess how much interest there would be from the Yorkshire Dales business community in participating in the project.

Activities

Explain that a ground-breaking project has been organised in the Yorkshire Dales National Park that attempts to use electric bicycles to boost tourism while cutting down on the negative effects of road traffic. Ask the pupils to study the press release issued by the project organisers in pairs and then complete the following activities.

Ⓔ Local use

Ask the pupils to identify two *benefits* and three *drawbacks* of local people using the electric bikes to get to their nearest settlements (e.g. towns like Grassington that have shops, a library, doctors etc.)

Ⓜ A day trip

Ask the pupils to plan a day-long excursion around the Wharfedale region of the Yorkshire Dales using the bikes, visiting some of the local attractions and facilities along the way. Provide maps and relevant tourist information to help the pupils plan the day.

Ⓒ Who would benefit most?

Ask the pupils to weigh up, from the list below, who would get the most out of an electric bike scheme:

- the residents of a hamlet such as Arncliffe where two electric bikes would be based

- visitors staying in a holiday cottage for a week

- residents of a large village with five bikes.

They should be prepared to explain their choice to the class as part of a wider debate.

Teacher's tips

- Provide a map of the Yorkshire Dales area so your pupils can become acquainted with the travel constraints in a rural area such as this (suitable maps are available from www.yorkshiredales.org.uk).

- The settlements of Buckden and Grassington can be explored by using the national park's virtual visits pages, which include 360-degree views:

  www.yorkshiredales.org.uk/outandabout/virtualvisits/vv-buckden/virtualvisit-buckden

  www.yorkshiredales.org.uk/outandabout/virtualvisits/vv-grassington/virtualvisit-grassington.

- Some of the smaller settlements such as Arncliffe, Kettlewell and Kilnsey could be explored using Google StreetView.

Plenary

Pupil stimulus

Ask the pupils to imagine that an electric bike scheme is proposed for their local area (i.e. within 20 miles of your school).

Activity

E **M** **C** Your local area

Ask the pupils if they think a scheme such as this could work in their local area? They should explain whether, in their opinion, it would be more or less successful than in the Yorkshire Dales.

Teacher's tips

- Differentiation on the above task can be achieved by asking pupils to carefully weigh up the pros and cons of a scheme taking place locally, and more fully justify the reasons given in their final decision.

- It may help to explain that, for such schemes to work, you need to have a mix of bike hubs, charge points and mechanical backup (similar to a car roadside-recovery service).

- A bike hub would need a secure place to store the bikes and hire them from.

- A substantial investment is required in advance to set up a hub, as each bike costs just under £1,000 to buy (though the businesses can lease them from the Electric Bike Network for considerably less).

- The suggested hire tariff for tourists and local people is £30 per day.

- Battery-range anxiety is probably the biggest problem of the bikes. They will actually comfortably take you up to 30 miles, but the more effort you put into peddling the further the battery range is. A full charge would take two hours, but there is also the option just to top up while having a coffee.

- Mechanical backup would usually be provided by an existing bike shop. In the Yorkshire Dales there are already two mobile bike mechanics who will collect your bike and return it to your doorstep. Both these individuals expressed, at an early stage in the development of the project, their interest in providing roadside recovery for the electric bikes and this made the whole proposal viable.

Extension

These activities provide the launchpad for your pupils to find out more about the various Electric Bike Networks being set up across the UK, including the successful schemes in the Peak District and Lake District National Parks. They could also try to plan a small scheme in their local area, enabling them to better understand the challenges involved. It would be interesting for your pupils to explore what local business could offer as incentives for people to charge their batteries at their hubs. These could, for example, include spending £5 at a café, or getting a free charge while getting their hair cut.

Geographical skills can save your life!

Main topic: How geographical skills can help people in day-to-day life.

Additional topic: The need for preparation when venturing outdoors.

Key geographical questions:

- How can geographical skills help people stay safe when exploring the outdoors?

- What geographical skills can be used by people in other aspects of their leisure time?

Online resources: Mountain Rescue service information card.

Although these activities can be used any time during a geography course, they would probably work best if they were carried out after pupils have gained an understanding of some of the diverse skills that the subject of geography offers.

Starter

Pupil stimulus

The Mountain Rescue Service in the Yorkshire Dales recently issued a special information card to remind visitors what they need to do to ensure they stay safe while out on the fells. This development was partly in response to numerous call-outs to people who were lost or got into difficulty while out in the Yorkshire Dales – usually because they were poorly prepared for the outdoors. The aim of the information cards was to encourage people to think carefully about the preparation needed to head outdoors safely and the skills that are needed once in the open air. Show the pupils the information card which can be found online.

Activities
❷ Skills

Ask the pupils to think about what skills, learnt by geography pupils studying at school, can help people stay safe while outdoors in the countryside?

Ⓜ Advice

Ask the pupils which piece of advice contained on the information card has *most* relevance to geography pupils and why?

Ⓒ Who should pay?

Some argue that if people are reckless and get themselves into difficulties in the countryside, they should pay for the efforts of the mountain rescue services who locate them and lead them to safety. To what extent do the pupils agree with this view?

> ### Teacher's tip
>
> It should be explained to pupils that the UK's mountain rescue services are staffed by hard-working and often heroic volunteers, although they do get grants from the government and also benefit from local fundraising activities. The highly-skilled rescue teams include expert geographers who are experienced in tracking and 'micro-navigation' – often aided by specially-trained tracker dogs.

Plenary

Pupil stimulus

The skills learnt by geography pupils are not just relevant to time spent in the countryside, they apply to many other aspects of everyday life. In this activity the pupils will be asked to think about some of these.

Activities

Ⓔ Leisure time

Ask the pupils to name three other ways in which geographical skills can be used during leisure time.

Ⓜ Sport

In small groups, ask the pupils to discuss the idea that geographical skills can be used by people who play *sport* in their leisure time. They should try to identify five ways in which people who play sport can benefit from having geographical skills.

ⓒ Countryside managers

Some people have argued that geography should be dropped from the curriculum to make room for other subjects such as information technology or business studies. Ask the pupils to think about why could this create problems for countryside managers, such as the people who manage national parks?

Teacher's tip

You may wish to carry out a thought-showering exercise before pupils begin these activities to help them see the range of geographical skills that might be used in daily life. Pupils often take the skills they learn at school for granted and overlook their use beyond the school gate.

Extension

These activities would be an excellent prelude to the production of a poster for display in your school entitled something like 'Geography – learning about our world / learning important skills to live better in the world'. This could be used on options evenings to draw pupils' and parents/carers' attention to some of the positive aspects of geography as a subject. Such posters are more authentic if they include the contributions of pupils, so you should ensure that these are included prominently for all to see.

Glastonbury divides opinion

Main topic: Rural development.

Additional topics: Diversification in the countryside; conflicts with visitors in rural areas.

Key geographical question: What are the pros and cons of major public events that take place in the countryside?

These activities can used be used flexibly, but are best introduced in the weeks running up to the Glastonbury Festival, which takes place in the last week of June.

Starter

Pupil stimulus

The legendary Glastonbury Festival of Contemporary Performing Arts, usually known simply as 'Glastonbury Festival', is the world's largest greenfield festival, attracting 175,000 visitors to its farmland base in Somerset, England in June every year.

The festival, which first took place in 1970, has attracted almost all of the world's biggest music acts – including many of the most iconic bands and soloists of the last 40 years. Tickets for the annual event often sell out on the first day they are issued, and hundreds of businesses benefit from the festival by providing a wide range of products and services for visitors, including food stalls, bars, clothing outlets, jewellery tents and a wide range of other attractions.

The Glastonbury Festival is not without its critics, however, and many people have pointed out that the festival site and the area around it are adversely affected by the thousands of visitors who descend on the site every year. Surrounding villages and access roads become clogged with cars, camper vans and buses and there is a huge logistical operation to dispose of the vast amounts of waste produced at the site by the thousands of revellers. If the rain falls, conditions underfoot become incredibly muddy, so much so that festival goers often leave the site caked in mud from head to foot – and leave muddy trails from their festival wellies much of the way back to their homes all over the country.

Some people have begun to ask the question of whether the Glastonbury Music Festival should be allowed to continue given the pressure it exerts on a scenic part of Somerset.

Activities
ⓔ Benefits

Ask the pupils to consider what are the benefits of the Glastonbury Festival to the festival goers and the people providing support services on the festival site?

ⓜ Benefits and negatives

Ask the pupils to make a list of five benefits of the Glastonbury Festival and five negative points about it.

ⓖ Should it continue?

Ask the pupils to weigh up the evidence for and against the continuation of the Glastonbury Festival and try to come to a conclusion about whether it should continue.

> ### Teacher's tip
>
> The degree of interest your pupils are likely to show in the Glastonbury Festival is likely to be linked to their age, with older pupils likely to be more avid followers of the event. Having said that, popular music is, of course, one of the things that binds young people together and every year group is likely to find the topic to be 'cool' and engaging compared to many other areas of the curriculum.

Plenary

Pupil stimulus

Glastonbury Festival is just one example of an event that brings *conflict* to the countryside in one part of the UK. There are, of course, many other types of conflict affecting the countryside, stemming from a whole range of causes. Each of these needs a special set of responses in order to try and find an outcome that satisfies all the interested parties. Sometimes, of course, it is not possible to please everyone.

Activities
ⓔ Conflict in the countryside

Ask the pupils to identify another conflict taking place in the countryside and state clearly who the different parties are.

Ⓜ Why does it occur?

Ask the pupils to identify two different types of conflict that can occur in the countryside and for each explain why each conflict occurs.

Ⓒ Hard to resolve

Ask the pupils to give an example of a conflict in the countryside that has been especially difficult to resolve and explain why this conflict proved to be particularly challenging.

Teacher's tip

Pupils living in rural areas are more likely to be familiar with specific conflicts in the countryside than those based in more urban settings. It may be appropriate to provide a range of examples in the form of concise summaries on postcard-sized cards for any pupils who are short of ideas.

Extension

The theme of *conflict* is a particularly important one in geography, which crops up in a very wide range of topic areas. To help pupils draw the different strands of conflict together, draw a mind-map showing the common types of conflicts (e.g. conflicts between different groups of people and their particular interests; between people and the environment; between short-term and long-term interests etc.) and the links between them. Creating such knowledge maps is important in allowing pupils to integrate new ideas on geographical conflicts into their existing knowledge frameworks.

Re-wilding the countryside

Main topic: Understanding how distinctive human and physical landscapes change over time.

Additional topic: The importance of an understanding of the interrelatedness of human activity and the landscape.

Key geographical questions:

- Is it possible for the effects of human industrial and commercial activity in the past to be reversed?

- What would be the impact of such conservation activity on the areas concerned?

Online resources: Printable pupil stimulus material.

These activities will help to generate discussion about the landscape in general and the impact of human activity, for good or for ill, upon the shape and appearance of that landscape. The point can be made that these impacts are as noticeable in the rural landscape as they are in the urban, but one has to look with a geographer's eye to see them.

Starter

In preparation for this it would be valuable to show the pupils this short video of a talk by George Monbiot at: http://vimeo.com/68575611.

Pupil stimulus

Provide pupils with a copy of the information 'Re-wilding', which is also available online.

Re-wilding

This is a term coined in 2011 by those who love and defend the natural world. It can be taken to mean the principle of allowing the world to return to its natural state.

Changes in the landscape
Human activity is responsible for making radical changes to the landscape; that is an observable fact. It is fascinating to look at old maps of your area and see the changes that have taken place over the years. Human activity has transformed all landscapes,

rural and urban. Much of what we think of as countryside is very heavily managed and nothing like what it would be if left to its own devices.

Mining and industry
This is very destructive of the landscape. However, since the closure of many collieries and other sites of heavy industry across Britain, formerly devastated areas have been painstakingly reclaimed to provide regenerated habitats.

Organisations such as the Royal Society for the Protection of Birds (RSPB) have established thriving nature reserves, these are havens for wildlife where visitors can learn about the plants, birds and other animals that have re-established themselves.

Intensive farming
Intensive farming practices have changed the landscape. We mostly see this in the way hedgerows have been taken down to create huge fields that can be worked more easily with today's modern farm machinery.

Initiatives exist to encourage farmers to leave hedgerows and make the field margins wider. This helps to create areas for plants and insects and so increases biodiversity; they also provide wildlife corridors for the movement of creatures around their ranges.

Hunting, shooting and fishing
In the past many rivers were straightened or weirs were put in to create artificial pools. This was to make them better for trout fishing. The vegetation of large tracts of upland moors is managed to provide the right habitat for red grouse.

Re-wilding projects have been set up to put the bends back into rivers and make them more attractive as habitats for a wider variety of native species. There are woodland areas where careful management of these complex habitats have made them richer and more diverse.

Activities

❺ What's good about a nature reserve?

Ask the pupils to look at the website for the RSPB reserve at Fairburn Ings in West Yorkshire (see below). On a piece of paper they should make two columns headed 'Wildlife' and 'Humans'. Ask them to discuss with a partner the good things that this place has and note them down in the appropriate column.

ⓜ Re-wilding – a new kind of land management

Ask the pupils to look carefully at both of the links below. They are describing similar projects, one in the Netherlands and the other in the UK. With a partner they should make a note of the essential similarities of the two schemes; and then note the essential differences.

The River Adur re-wilding scheme:
Go to: www.royalhaskoning.co.uk and search 'River Adur'.

The Oostvaardersplassen:
http://www.staatsbosbeheer.nl/English/Oostvaardersplassen.aspx

❻ The essential changes

Ask the pupils to consider what is the value of a re-wilding project? They should look at the links above and discuss how well the information makes the case for the re-wilding of these areas. Do they think that this is something that should be repeated elsewhere? Ask them to discuss these issues with a partner and make notes that can be shared with the class.

Teacher's tip

The urban built environment is one with which we are all familiar; this is a human construct. Also obvious is the impact of sheep farming on the vegetation of the downs and, critically, other hill areas. The direct influence of human activity over time can also be seen in other landscapes, such as human interference with rivers to create trout pools and streams for sport; the overpopulation of deer and the impact of management practices on grouse moors. This series of activities can be used to show that there is much being done to re-wild certain areas by looking carefully at land management in a new and more sustainable way. There is also a chance to discuss the issue of the restoration of land once abused by industry and thought to be derelict.

Forestry Commission home page:
http://www.forestry.gov.uk/website/fchomepages.nsf/hp/England

Woodland management page:
http://www.forestry.gov.uk/forestry/INFD-8M6E9E

Trees and climate change in formation pack
http://www.forestry.gov.uk/forestry/infd-8n7jkx

Fairburn Ings – an RSPB reserve on the site of an abandoned coal mine:
http://www.rspb.org.uk/reserves/guide/f/fairburnings/about.aspx

Plenary

Pupil stimulus

An opinion

If we take the idea of re-wilding to its natural conclusion there would have to be very few hill farmers. Much of the land they farm would be allowed to recover to open woodland suitable for wolf, lynx and perhaps bears could re-establish territories for themselves. The deer that are also currently destroying the hillside vegetation would be the prey of these carnivores and so they would not need to be controlled by shooting. The balance of nature would be restored. The reintroduction of wolves into the Yellowstone National Park in the USA had the effect of improving the entire ecosystem of the area.

Details of this project can be seen at: http://www.yellowstone-bearman.com/wolves.html

Activities

Ⓔ Fields without sheep

Ask the pupils to imagine there were no sheep in the fields. What would happen to the landscape in ten years?

Ⓜ Fear of predators

Humans are naturally afraid of predators – but we are predators ourselves. Ask the pupils to think about what predatory behaviours we show now – are they justified?

Ⓒ Fear

Why do the pupils think game-keepers and farmers are mostly against the reintroduction of predator species?

Extension

Re-wilding Europe

Re-wilding is a position taken by some conservation biologists and the impact in Europe of this movement can be seen at http://www.rewildingeurope.com/. Ask the pupils to examine the ideas presented in this website and decide what you feel about the re-wilding of Europe.

Section 5

Resource management

Rivers and their management

Main topic: River management.

Additional topic: Hydrological processes.

Key geographical question: What are the main management issues along rivers?

These activities should be used at the end of a unit of work on rivers and how people manage them.

Starter

Pupil stimulus

For this task, on the topic of rivers, the pupils will need to use their memory and imagination rather than relying on any resources you will give them. Explain to them that their memory/imagination can actually be very powerful tools to help them think about geographical issues. When they use their memory/imagination successfully they will get the satisfaction of knowing that they have solved the problem on their own.

Activities
Ⓔ A good question

Using the knowledge they have gained so far during their geography studies, ask the pupils to identify any *question* that geography pupils might ask about rivers. Ask them to share their question with a learning partner and tell them why they think this is a good question to ask about rivers.

Ⓜ Interacting with rivers

Using the knowledge they have gained so far during their geography studies, ask the pupils to identify two questions that geography pupils might ask about how people interact with rivers. Ask them to share their questions with a learning partner and suggest which of them is most relevant to the place where they live.

❻ Managing rivers

Using the knowledge they have gained so far during their geography studies, ask the pupils to identify three questions that geography pupils might ask about how people manage rivers. Ask them to share their questions with a learning partner and ask them to rank the questions in order of how costly each type of management is likely to be.

Teacher's tips

- These tasks could prove rather challenging for some pupils because of the lack of external stimuli, which can leave pupils feeling a little 'exposed'. You should boost their confidence by reassuring them that they *can* answer the questions properly using only what they already know, combined with their imagination.

- In order to get in a good frame of mind for creative thinking, you may want to carry out some sort of 'brain-break' type of activity with your pupils before embarking on these tasks (for example light physical exercise or a short meditation period). In particular, you should try to help your pupils free their minds of clutter and be open to the surfacing of new ideas.

Plenary

Pupil stimulus

As with the starter, there is no additional stimulus for the plenary, which takes the topic of river management further. The plenary asks pupils to consider river management issues close to where they live.

Activities

❸ What have people done?

Ask the pupils to choose a river near to where they live and write a list of all the ways they can think of that people have affected this river – in positive as well as negative ways.

ⓂMajor management project

Ask the pupils to think about a river in their home area where people have carried out a *major* management project. Working in small groups, they should explain what was done and why they think the project was carried out.

● Mistakes of the past

Some river specialists have said that a lot of river management today is simply undoing the mistakes of the past. Ask the pupils what evidence there is from their home area to support this view.

Teacher's tips

- Pupils may appreciate some clarification over what constitutes *management*, as the range of possible measures is very broad.

- If pupils are struggling to identify local river management case studies, you could point them in the direction of a suitable example further afield that they are likely to know about.

Extension

These starter/plenary activities would lead naturally on to some extended project work looking at a specific river basin and how it has been managed over the generations. It would be most enriching for pupils if this case study were taken from a part of the world that they have so far studied only superficially, or preferably not at all. Most pupils really enjoy project work of this sort, which allows them to use their research skills and creativity to produce something tangible.

The fracas about fracking

Main topic: Mining for fossil fuels.

Additional topics: Power generation and supply.

Key geographical questions:

- What do we need to know about fracking to judge whether it is a safe way to extract gas from the ground?

- What should the energy mix be in order to meet the energy needs of the UK?

Online resources: Newspaper article, 'Communities get fractious about drilling for shale gas'.

Although this entry is a good way in to any unit of work on energy, the subject of fracking is a relatively new one in a UK context and many pupils (and indeed the wider community) may be unfamiliar with the key ideas, unless your school is situated in one of the test drilling areas.

Its novelty would make it a suitable subject to cover at the end of a period studying energy, as an example of a potential solution to the energy supply problem in the UK.

Starter

Pupil stimulus

Provide the pupils with a newspaper article, which you can download from the online resources, that looks at some of the issues surrounding drilling for shale gas.

Activities
❸ Facts about fracking

Ask the pupils to read the newspaper article with a learning partner and highlight any facts that would help to them to decide whether fracking is a good idea here in the UK.

Ⓜ Pros and cons

Ask the pupils to study the newspaper article and make a table showing the pros and cons of fracking. They should add any other points based on what they have heard on the news etc.

Ⓒ Scientific data

It is difficult to decide whether fracking for shale gas is a safe method of gas extraction owing to the lack of scientific information. Working with a learning partner, ask the pupils to identify at least five pieces of scientific data that would help make a more informed judgement.

Teacher's tip

The topic of fracking is new to many teachers and it would be a good idea to spend some time researching the subject before launching into any lessons that touch on it. Some of the views expressed by the protesters featured in the news are sensationalist and should be treated with caution.

Plenary

Activities

Ⓔ Other energy sources

Shale gas is just one of several energy sources used to generate electricity in the UK. Ask the pupils to make a list of all the other energy sources they can think of.

Ⓜ Non-renewable and renewable energy

Ask the pupils to draw a two-columned table and put 'non-renewable' and 'renewable' at the top of the columns. They should then list as many different energy sources as they can in the correct column – for example shale gas is a non-renewable energy type, so it goes in that column.

Ⓒ Pie chart

Ask the pupils to work with a learning partner to draw a pie chart that shows what they think the most appropriate mix of energy sources should be in the UK. They should add labels to explain and justify each segment.

Teacher's tip

If you feel your pupils need to recap the various energy sources used in the UK (and whether they class as non-renewable or renewable) draw a mind-map on the whiteboard to illustrate this, taking ideas from those pupils who can remember key facts.

Extension

Power generation is a major topic within geography, even just in a UK context, and is set to become even more significant as the world's population increases and fossil fuel reserves begin to run out. You can take things further by asking pupils to carry out a piece of extended project work that reviews the pros and cons of all the major power production methods used in the UK. They can present the results in a report that also recommends which energy sources have the most potential in this country.

Water, the essence of life

Main topic: The link between the plentiful supply of safe water and the health of a community.

Key geographical questions:

• Is it a human right to have access to safe drinking water?

• What measures are in place to improve water supply?

Online resources: Video link; printable pupil stimulus material; 'Water, the essence of life' worksheet.

Any discussion about the health and well-being of populations will have to focus on the availability of safe and affordable drinking water and effective sanitation. The importance of water to the whole life of the planet cannot be overstated. Water security and the control of supply is already impacting on the politics of some areas, particularly in north east Africa.

This series of activities looks at a specific intervention in Nicaragua to allow the pupils to investigate some of the facts and how in More Economically Developed Countries (MEDCs) we take the seemingly endless supply of water on tap for granted.

Starter

Pupil stimulus

Information for this task is in the short video found at (a clickable link can also be found online): http://www.wateraid.org/where-we-work/page/nicaragua#/djvBzxu5TiA

Ask the pupils to watch it a couple of times and make notes. They will need to work together on this task and make decisions based on their understanding of the information in the film.

Activities

A pupil response sheet 'Water, the essence of life', which has the questions below and spaces for the answers, can be downloaded from the online resources for this book.

❸ Nicaragua

Why do you think that this area of Nicaragua is called the Mosquito Coast? What problem does this suggest to you might be there?

❸ The project

Write down six key facts that you find out from the film about the WaterAid project in Nicaragua and why it is important.

Ⓜ Water quality

Why is WaterAid promoting the use of wells and rain-water harvesting when this is not an arid country and there is plenty of surface water?

Ⓜ Technology

What are the main values of the use of 'low-tech' equipment such as the 'rope-pump'? Why could solar panels by useful?

❻ Immediate benefits

What do you think are the key impacts of this project on the lives of all the people in the area?

❻ Lasting impact

What are the features of this project that make it sustainable in this area? What would you imagine would be the situation in five or six years' time?

Teacher's tip

This task works best if the pupils are in twos or threes allowing for the cross-fertilisation and sharing of ideas. The completed grids can be compared and discussed as all the questions require some measure of judgement and opinion.

Plenary

Pupil stimulus

Provide the pupils with the following facts.

Did you know that...

- 768 million people (one in ten of the world's population) do not have easy access to safe drinking water?

- 40% of the world's population (2.5 billion) do not have access to adequate sanitation?

- Approximately 700,000 children die each year from diarrhoea caused by drinking or bathing in water contaminated by sewage?

(Figures from WaterAid UK)

Diseases

Cholera was a disease common in the cities of the UK until the latter part of the 19th century. In the late summer of 1854 there was a cholera outbreak in Soho, central London that claimed the lives of over 600 people.

The source of the infection

A doctor working in the area, John Snow, discovered that the source of the disease was drinking water from the public pump in Broad Street that had come in to contact with raw sewage. There were no proper sewers in that part of London at that time and it was easy for clean water and contaminated water to become mixed.

Understanding

At that time there was little understanding of the science of diseases and how they were transmitted. John Snow helped to move that understanding on. As we now know about the importance of clean running water to health why do so many people suffer so much through lack of it?

Activities

⊕ Water supply in the UK

From what they have seen on the video and the pupil stimulus information, ask the pupils to work with a learning partner to note down the three most important things about our water supply that we take for granted.

Ⓜ Where does it come from?

There are places in the world where water is very scarce, for example Dubai on the Persian Gulf coast and Las Vegas, the gambling capital of the USA, which is in the middle of the Nevada Desert. These are both thriving places. Ask the pupils how they think these places manage for water?

Ⓖ Water quality

We now have a greater understanding of the nature of water-borne diseases than in the past so why do the pupils think there are so many people who are unable to enjoy the benefits of fresh, safe water?

Teacher's tip

The work of John Snow in relation to the Soho cholera outbreak is well documented. The critical understanding that Snow achieved was that 'foul air' was not the cause of disease, but something else carried in the water. This is before Pasteur's germ theory (1861) had been developed. This task asks the pupils to think about the link between clean water and well-being and how the inequalities that exist across the world in that respect are to do with things other than scientific knowledge.

Extension

Explore the low-tech approaches to the delivery of clean water in LICs. This can be done through http://www.wateraid.org/uk/what-we-do/our-approach/delivering-services

Ask the pupils to look at the techniques below, which are illustrated online, and evaluate each of them in terms of their cost and their long-term and sustainable use:

• bore-hole drilling

• the rope pump

• rainwater harvesting

• the gravity flow system

• the gulper.

New trends in 21st century tourism

Main topic: The impacts of tourism on people, property and environment.

Additional topic: Economic development and inequality.

Key geographical question: What are the pros and cons of 'The World', a major offshore tourist site in Dubai?

Online resources: Printable pupil stimulus material.

These activities would work equally well at the beginning, middle or end of a unit of work on tourism.

Starter

Pupil stimulus

Provide the pupils with the information about 'The World' resort below.

'The World' rises from the ocean

An extraordinary construction project is currently taking place off the coast of Dubai, one of the seven emirates that make up the very wealthy country of the United Arab Emirates, situated in the Middle East. Hundreds of islands are being built two and a half miles from the coastline to create one of the world's most incredible tourist resorts and holiday destinations. The most amazing aspect of the development, however, is only visible from the air: the islands have been laid out to recreate the shape of the world's continents and countries – so much so that the development has been called 'The World'!

When it is fully completed, the complex will be home to luxury hotels and sporting facilities. Rich sun-seekers will also have the option to purchase whole islands so they can build exclusive holiday homes on them, with islands ranging in size from 14,000 to 42,000 square metres in size. The starting prices for such a purchase are spectacular, with the smallest island costing millions of pounds. This has led several celebrities to buy islands in the hope that they can find some peace and quiet in 'The World', away from paparazzi photographers and autograph hunters. It has even been rumoured that David and Victoria

Beckham have shown interest in buying the whole of 'Europe' on which they hope to build a huge holiday villa for themselves and their four children.

This massive development has brought many changes to Dubai, some positive and others not so positive. Although the project has created thousands of jobs, providing employment for construction workers, labourers, landscape gardeners and many other types of workers, some local people have not been happy because they say most of the workers have been shipped in from overseas. Although the workers themselves are not keen to talk about their working and living conditions for fear of losing their jobs, evidence has emerged to suggest that wages are very low and living conditions cramped, dirty and sometimes unsafe.

The development has brought benefits further afield, with several British companies having been awarded lucrative contracts to work on the project, including those specialising in underwater construction and the planning of large leisure resorts. Being associated with this important development has also helped these companies build their international profile.

The project is set to bring millions of pounds of new income into the Dubai economy, and will create thousands of permanent new jobs when fully open – mostly for local people. Yet despite already costing £10 billion to construct, only two of the islands have permanent buildings on them. There have also been concerns from environmentalists that the development will spoil the habitat of several types of exotic fish and could even disturb important sea-bird feeding areas. More recently, unconfirmed reports have claimed that the islands, which are constructed of sand dredged from Dubai's shallow coastal waters, are sinking back into the sea. This, together with the fact that the global financial crisis (which began in 2008) has delayed the development of the islands, means that their future is currently uncertain.

Activities

Ⓔ A good thing?

Ask the pupils to explain why 'The World' development will be a good thing for Dubai.

Ⓜ Different perspectives

Ask the pupils to make a list of the pros and cons of 'The World' development from the perspective of an overseas construction worker and a resident of Dubai.

Ⓖ Should it be halted?

Ask the pupils how realistic it would be to argue that 'The World' development should be halted because of its effects on the ecology of the marine ecosystem? Ask them to make sure that they fully justify their answer.

Teacher's tips

- There are some impressive images online of the amazing islands of 'The World', which you should show your pupils to give them a sense of the immense scale and visually striking nature of this flagship project (see www.privateislandsonline.com/islands/the-world-islands-dubai).

- Your pupils may touch upon the kudos the Dubai government will gain from the completion of such a visionary and ground-breaking project, which is a genuine world first. You may, in turn, wish to introduce them to the concept of 'vanity construction projects' – major, headline-grabbing developments that are carried out as much to massage the egos of billionaire business-people or politicians, as they are to benefit local people.

Plenary

Pupil stimulus

Visitor managers in some forward-thinking tourist locations in the UK have published sustainable development plans that explain what will be done to strike a better balance between the needs of people and the environment. They have also drawn up these plans in the hope that visitors will be able to make more informed choices about their own impact on the environment while on holiday. The hope is that in time all the major tourist locations in the UK (and eventually overseas) will have their own sustainable development plan, which will have a hugely positive impact on the environment.

Activities

Ⓔ Sustainable development plan

Ask the pupils to identify five things that would go into a sustainable development plan for a tourist destination they have visited. They should then discuss this with a learning partner.

Ⓜ Reduce, re-use and recycle

The slogan 'Reduce, re-use and recycle' can be applied to sustainable development plans for tourist areas. Ask the pupils to draw a three-columned table and write in it the ways people can reduce, re-use and recycle as part of a sustainable development plan for tourism.

❻ Measures in place

Ask the pupils to think about a tourist destination they have visited in the last few years. What evidence did they see during their visit that suggested measures to promote sustainable development have already started?

Teacher's tips

- Many pupils will enjoy telling others where they have been on holiday and you could start with a 'show and tell' session where they bring in postcards, photos, tourist-trinkets etc. to bring their holiday stories to life.

- If pupils are struggling to imagine the full scope of a sustainable development plan for tourism, encourage them to think about the following topics: impact on the built environment; impact on water supply; managing waste; impact on the atmosphere; impact on the soil; impact on natural ecosystems and individual species.

Extension

Most pupils enjoy designing posters and this enthusiasm can be harnessed by asking them to design an advert for a bed and breakfast establishment or hotel that is situated in a leading area for environmentally-conscious tourism. The aim of the poster is to stress the measures that are being taken by the business to reduce the negative impacts of tourism on the local environment.

A high price for gemstones and precious metals?

Main topic: Physical and human processes.

Additional topics: Environmental action and sustainable development; place.

Key geographical questions:

- Why are people attracted to gemstone mining in poor countries such as Madagascar?

- How can the mining of rubies and other gemstones in Madagascar damage the environment of the extraction sites?

Online resources: Gemstone mining magazine article.

This activity encourages pupils to consider the human and environmental issues surrounding the extraction of gemstones on the Indian Ocean island of Madagascar. There is also a creative exercise that challenges pupils to think about the implications of gold mining in Wales, a country much wealthier than Madagascar. The activity would work well as an introduction to extractive industries, which continue to be a very important part of the economy of many countries.

Starter

Pupil stimulus

Show pupils the magazine article from the online resources which explains the importance of gemstone mining in Madagascar.

Activities

E Searching for gems

Ask the pupils why do so many Malagasy people want to look for gems in the rivers and caves of their country?

Ⓜ Environmental effects

Ask the pupils what environmental effects are miners having on the area where the gems occur?

Ⓒ Code of conduct

A code of conduct for gemstone miners could help to reduce the negative effects of mining. Can the pupils identify between three and five things that could be included in such a code of conduct?

Teacher's tips

• Some Madagascar facts should be shared with the pupils as context, including its status as the world's fourth largest island and its location in the Indian Ocean to the east of Africa.

• Rubies make a fascinating subject to study due to their comparative rarity, high value and incredible hardness (third only to diamonds and moissanite). Explain their importance in jewellery making, including their link to the British Royal Family, as well as giving some background to their formation and structure.

• Encourage pupils to make a connection with mining activities in their home region. Why is it done and what are the environmental consequences?

• If pupils are finding the 'Challenging' task too difficult, encourage them to join up with a partner to pool ideas.

Plenary

Pupil stimulus

In the UK there are no deposits of gemstones such as rubies or diamonds. However, in the past gold was mined in several areas of the country, especially in Scotland and Wales. Even today, it is still possible to find specks of river gold in a few secret locations by carefully 'panning' the sediment.

Activities

Ⓜ Gold rush!

Ask the pupils to imagine that a major new source of gold is discovered in one of the principal rivers of the Snowdonia Mountains in North Wales. What would the local authorities need to do to make sure that large numbers of 'gold-hunters' did not overrun the area and cause lasting damage to the environment?

Teacher's tips

- You can help bring this activity alive by showing pupils images of some of the beautiful historic artefacts made of gold that have been found buried in the ground in the UK. These include several 'hoards' of metalwork, jewellery and coins that amateurs have unearthed, some of which are worth hundreds of thousands of pounds (see, for example, http://www.britishmuseum.org/explore/highlights/highlight_objects/pe_prb/t/the_great_torc_from_snettisham.aspx, http://en.wikipedia.org/wiki/Staffordshire_Hoard, and http://www.dailymail.co.uk/news/article-2336423/I-Roman-coins-worth-100-000—20-minutes-buying-metal-detector-Novice-unearths-nationally-significant-treasure-hunt.html).

- Pupils would find it useful to study the main events of the 1849 US gold-rush and the manner in which the discovery of gold gripped the nation (see, for example, http://www.history.com/topics/gold-rush-of-1849, http://www.history.com/topics/gold-rush-of-1849 and http://en.wikipedia.org/wiki/California_Gold_Rush).

Extension

Ask the pupils to prepare a short PowerPoint presentation showing how people benefit from one substance that is mined in Europe.

Section 6
Natural hazards

Dealing with an increasingly flooded world

Main topic: Physical and human processes.

Additional topics: Place; geographical enquiry.

Key geographical questions:

• What were the effects of the June 2012 Calderdale flood in Yorkshire?

• What can we do to reduce flooding in river valleys such as Calderdale?

Online resources: Calderdale flood article; x2 flood photos, one in Calderdale and one in Dhaka.

This entry would provide an engaging introduction to a unit of work on natural hazards, or the study of a river and its effects on its drainage basin. Most pupils are motivated by the dramatic spectacle of a natural hazard caught on film, and there are some excellent video clips on YouTube of the Calderdale 2012 floods to view with them (the compilation of nine clips entitled 'Hebden Bridge floods 2012' is particularly good, though there are many other useful clips of the event on this site).

Starter

Pupil stimulus

Following serious floods in the Calderdale area of West Yorkshire in June 2012, the Environment Agency published some information on its website to help explain what happened (see online resources). The Environment Agency is the government body responsible for flood management in the UK.

Activities

Ask the pupils to read the extract from the Environment Agency website about the Calderdale flood before completing the following activities.

Ⓔ Looking at the facts

Ask the pupils what facts about the flood show it was a serious flood event?

ⓂWhat were the effects?

Ask the pupils to describe the effects the flood would have had on homes, property and businesses in the Calder valley.

ⒸDid they do enough?

Some local people have said that the Environment Agency have not done enough to prevent floods happening in Calderdale. What information do the pupils think would need to be collected to find out whether this view can be backed up with reliable evidence?

Teacher's tips

- Make sure pupils have the chance to study the geography of the Calder valley before they begin work on the tasks, including its relation to major settlements such as Manchester, Huddersfield and Bradford and the network of major rivers and streams in the area.

- The 'Challenging' task is an especially challenging activity which requires pupils to think about specific information that would need to be collected in order to make a judgement about the effectiveness of the flood management measures taken to date. It is an ideal activity for more able pupils.

- At the end of the starter period bring together some of the key ideas by asking three pupils (one who has worked on each task) to share their answers. As you do this, add in any key ideas that the pupils do not mention.

Plenary

Pupil stimulus

The UK is, of course, not alone in being affected by floods. Indeed, flooding is one of the most widespread natural hazards affecting most countries in the world. In some countries floods cause much more damage than in the UK, and are responsible for high levels of deaths and injury. The Asian country of Bangladesh, where many people live in a vast lowland delta, is one example of a country that endures catastrophic floods on a regular basis. Show the pupils the photograph (see online resources) of a flood scene in Dhaka, Bangladesh's capital city.

Activities

Ⓔ Flooding around the world

Ask the pupils if they can say where else in the world have people been severely affected by floods? Ask them to name at least three countries.

Ⓜ The different effects

Ask the pupils to make a list of the various effects that floods have on people, property and the environment.

Ⓒ Why are there different impacts?

Ask the pupils why, in poor countries such as Bangladesh, do floods tend to kill more people than in rich countries such as the UK?

Teacher's tips

- When discussing the answers to the 'Easy' task with the pupils, make sure that at least three different countries are mentioned to give a good geographical spread.

- Provide verbal prompts as pupils work on the 'Challenging' task to help them find appropriate responses, including: What are the buildings like? What are medical services like? How well equipped are the emergency services? How good is the road system? How easy is it for people to be warned about the floods?

- Provide a thought-provoking end to the lesson by asking pupils how long they think it will be before death rates from floods in countries such as Bangladesh will be brought down to an acceptable level. What specific changes will need to take place for this to happen?

Extension

Every year, the UK government spends millions of pounds on flood prevention work along rivers to prevent houses and businesses being damaged in flooding incidents. Despite this investment, floods continue to cause damage to property in places such as Calderdale. Ask the pupils to prepare a 200-word statement explaining why it is impossible to prevent *every* flood from occurring. The statement should be suitable for being read out at a public meeting of residents and business owners concerned about flood risk in their area.

Natural hazards and their effects on people, property and the environment

Main topic: Physical and human processes.

Additional topic: Place.

Key geographical questions:

- Why is it so important for people living in earthquake zones to be prepared for earthquakes?

- What kind of precautions can be taken to reduce the impact of earthquakes?

Online resources: An earthquake witness account; a photo of earthquake damage.

This entry allows pupils to learn more about a series of earthquakes that affected a part of Italy that is not normally associated with serious earthquakes. As well being used as a case study of a specific earthquake event, the entry can also be used to explore the tectonic processes in the Mediterranean region that give rise to earthquakes. The inclusion of real-life testimony from an eye witness makes the emotional and physical effects of such earthquakes clear.

Starter

Pupil stimulus

Emily Rizzo (age nine) lives near the town of Este in Veneto province, north-east Italy. In May 2012 this part of Italy witnessed a number of earthquakes. Emily gives her account of one of these earthquakes in the extract that can be found online.

Activities

Ask the pupils to read Emily's account of the earthquake that affected her school before completing the tasks below.

🄴 Preparation

Ask the pupils to consider in what ways was Emily's school not prepared for the earthquake?

Ⓜ Lack of planning

Ask the pupils to consider what were the results of this lack of planning for school staff, children and parents?

🄶 What should be done

Ask the pupils to write a five-point reminder for the headteachers of schools in earthquake zones in Italy, advising what they should do to prepare for future quakes.

Teacher's tips

- Begin the activity by getting pupils to locate the area in Italy affected by the earthquakes. They could plot on the map any places they have heard of (e.g. major cities, places where football teams play etc.).

- To help pupils understand the concept of preparedness, ask them to mention any equipment (e.g. tools, a torch, a first-aid kit), food/drink or other items their parents store safely for emergency situations.

- Show pupils the position of the earth's plates in southern Europe and explain how this gives rise to earthquakes

---

Plenary

Pupil stimulus

People in Japan are very aware of the earthquake risk in their country. The Japanese government has spent hundreds of millions of pounds to make sure home owners, schools and businesses are well prepared for any earthquakes. This has included:

- Strengthening buildings to make them less likely to collapse.

- Asking schools and businesses to prepare earthquake plans.

- Informing people of unusual activity in the earth's crust that could indicate an earthquake is about to occur.

- Having regular national and regional earthquake drills where emergency procedures are practised.

- Having highly-trained emergency services personnel ready to tackle fires, rescue people and get them to hospital in the event of an earthquake.

Activities

Ⓜ Natural hazards

Ask the pupils to identify a country that suffers from a natural hazard other than earthquakes. In what ways does the government in that country try to ensure that people are well prepared for the natural hazard?

Teacher's tips

- Less able pupils are likely to come up with a small range of examples.

- More able pupils are likely to identify a wider range of examples.

- When summing up this activity try to distinguish between the general state of preparedness of rich and poor countries and how this affects the impacts of any natural hazards.

Extension

Ask the pupils to produce a fact-file about a recent earthquake to include:

- The time, date and place of the earthquake.

- Its strength on the Richter Scale.

- The effects of the earthquake on people, property, businesses, services and the environment.

- Any lessons learnt from the earthquake and the response to it.

Huge meteor explodes in Russian atmosphere

Main topic: The effects of natural hazards on people, property and the environment.

Additional topic: Meteors as a natural hazard.

Key geographical questions:

- In what ways could the Russian meteor of 2012 be considered a natural hazard?

- How could we prepare for meteor explosions and impacts to reduce the effects on people, property and the environment?

Online resources: 2013 Chelyabinsk meteor air burst information sheet.

The topic of exploding meteors is an ideal subject to liven up any geography lesson and would be a spectacular way of starting a unit of work on natural hazards. The amazing video of the exploding Russian meteor, captured by members of the public (much of it still available on YouTube), should captivate even the most disaffected geography pupil.

Starter

Pupil stimulus

Natural hazards

Natural hazards are naturally-occurring phenomena that occur at, below or above the ground or water surface, that can be dangerous to people, property and the environment. They include Earth processes such as volcanoes, earthquakes and landslides, as well as atmospheric phenomena such as hurricanes, tornadoes and drought and water-based hazards such as tsunamis.

Provide the pupils with the information sheet (available from the online resources) about the 2013 Chelyabinsk meteor air burst before they complete the following activities. They can also watch the video clips of the 2012 Chelyabinsk meteor strike on the Wikipedia entry for this incident (http://en.wikipedia.org/wiki/Russian_Meteor).

Activities

ⓔ Effects on people

Ask the pupils: How did the Russian meteor affect the people where it exploded?

ⓜ Preparing for a meteor explosion

Ask the pupils: What could people do to prepare themselves for a meteor explosion, in order to reduce the potential impact?

ⓒ Is it cost-effective?

Meteor strikes and explosions are rare events on Earth that can be hard to predict. In view of this, do the pupils think it is cost-effective and sensible for people to invest in measures to reduce the risk they pose? Tell them they must justify their views with reference to at least *two* meteor explosions.

> ### Teacher's tips
>
> • The rarity of meteor explosions in the Earth's atmosphere probably means that your pupils will have limited understanding of the processes at work when a meteor enters the Earth's atmosphere. You should therefore make sure you give them enough background knowledge to make sense of the video clips and the other information they will come across about the meteor explosion. The Wikipedia page for the Chelyabinsk meteor (http://en.wikipedia.org/wiki/Russian_Meteor) is excellent and includes links to dramatic eyewitness video footage taken as the event unfolded.
>
> • A common misconception among pupils is that the meteors which penetrate our atmosphere are huge; the truth is that most of these meteors, including those that we can see as night-time shooting stars, are tiny objects no bigger than a marble (and are often only the size of a grain of sand!) that simply burn up as they pass through the upper atmosphere. The Chelyabinsk meteor was clearly an exception, and its 17-20 metre size meant it was capable of causing a huge amount of damage.

Plenary

Pupil stimulus

Natural hazards sometimes bring an unexpected benefit in the form of distinctive deposits that are left behind, which people can make use of. These include:

• Meteorites – pieces of meteor that have landed on the Earth's surface.

- Fulgurites – glass-like tubes of 'fossilised' soil or sediment created when lightning strikes at ground level.

- Tektites – small bodies with a glass-like appearance, formed when meteorites strike the Earth and eject large amounts of debris into the air (the tektites found on Earth are from ancient meteor impacts).

These rare deposits are highly prized by collectors, so some people try to find them on or in the ground so they can make money by selling them – often on the internet. At the time of writing there were 4,808 meteorites listed on UK eBay, with the most expensive 'Buy It Now' example costing £12,850! The high value of meteorites has led some people to sell fake pieces of the now notorious 2012 Russian meteorite – often at huge prices.

Activities

❷ Owning a meteorite

Ask the pupils: Why do you think people want to own meteorites and other unusual deposits produced by natural hazards?

ⓜ Snowy regions

Most meteorites are found in remote, snowy regions of the Arctic or Antarctic. Why do the pupils think that these are these good places for finding meteorites?

❸ A free market?

Ask the pupils: Do you think people should be allowed to collect and sell meteorites freely, or should they all be donated to museums so scientists can study them? They should fully explain the reasons for their answer.

> ### Teacher's tip
>
> It is important for your pupils to see examples of meteorites and the other deposits mentioned above – via projected images or even in the hand. Your local museum may have specimens they can lend you, and might even be able to send a member of staff to talk to your pupils and answer questions. Small pieces of fulgurite and tektites are often available at low cost (i.e. a few pounds) online or via rock/fossil shops.

Extension

London's Natural History Museum plays host to some of the world's finest meteorites, as well as a vast array of other geological oddities. A visit to this outstanding museum would be sure to amaze and inspire your pupils in equal measure. If this is logistically difficult, the museum's website (www.nhm.ac.uk) is an excellent place to enable your pupils to continue studying meteors and their effect on people. An interesting activity for your pupils to carry out when they have studied a range of natural hazards is to try and classify the hazards according to several different criteria, including:

- frequency of hazard

- impacts of hazard (on people, property and the environment)

- scale of impact of hazard (in most cases a range will need to be given)

- measures people can take to reduce the impacts (specific examples should be given)

- extent to which the measures to reduce the impacts can be successful.

The results of this classification exercise are best recorded in a matrix or table that can be added to as further information comes to light.

Section 7

Wildlife conservation and people

Looking after the local environment – the role of wildlife trusts

Main topic: Environmental interaction and sustainable development.

Additional topics: Place; space.

Key geographical questions:

- Why is it important that Britain's natural environment is preserved?

- What are people doing to achieve this?

Online resources: Printable pupil stimulus material; photograph of Attenborough Nature Centre.

This group of activities is designed to help to raise pupils' awareness of their natural environment, what is happening to preserve it at a local level and the interconnectedness of the different human and natural elements of the landscape at local level. The plenary features an example of a 'green building'.

Starter

Pupil stimulus

Below are the objectives from the Strategic Plan of a county Wildlife Trust – ask the pupils to read them carefully to make sure that they understand all the terms before completing the activities below.

Background

The Berks, Bucks and Oxon Wildlife Trust (BBOWT) is one of a network of 47 such trusts across the United Kingdom. Wildlife trusts are locally based volunteer organisations concerned with all aspects of nature conservation. This is an extract from the current BBOWT Strategic Plan.

> **Our strategic objectives**
>
> **Nature reserves:** to create and care for natural places as wildlife havens for people to enjoy.
>
> **Living landscapes:** to work in partnership to develop landscape-scale schemes to enable wildlife and people to thrive.
>
> **Engaging people:** to create new opportunities to enable everyone to gain access to and take action for wildlife.
>
> **Education:** to inspire the next generation to care for the natural world.
>
> **Championing wildlife:** to be an effective voice for wildlife at local and regional level
>
> From *Strategic Plan for 2010 – 2015*, p4, BBOWT.

Activities

❺ Interpreting the objectives

Ask the pupils to choose one of the objectives. In discussion with a learning partner they should decide what the objective means and write a sentence to show their interpretation of it.

Ⓜ Making decisions

Ask the pupils to look in detail at the list of objectives in the strategic plan and choose two of them. In discussion with their learning partner they should decide on four (or more) reasons why they think each of these objectives is important and write these down.

❻ A question of meaning

Ask the pupils to examine why the word *partnership* (in the 'Living landscapes' objective) might be very important to the success of that objective. Who might these partners be and why might they be interested? After discussing this with their learning partner they should write down a response that they can share with the class. If they have time they might also look at the word *engaging* in the 'Engaging people' objective and/or *education* in the 'Education' objective and define these words in the context of the strategic objectives.

> **Teacher's tips**
>
> * They key to these tasks is for the pupils to be comfortable with the terms and the concepts in the strategic objectives box as the tasks are asking them to approach both the vocabulary and the concepts surrounding some of the issues concerning the stewardship of the natural environment.

- The tasks are designed to be carried out in groups of two or three and each task demands a brief written response to help to keep focus. The responses could be written on sticky notes and put on display – part of the plenary could be for the class to look at the responses from the other groups in the class.

Plenary

Pupil stimulus

'Green building' is a term used to refer to the construction and function of buildings that are efficient in their use of energy, water, and other resources; they are healthy places to live or work in and they are designed specifically to reduce waste, pollution and impact upon the environment.

To achieve the objective of creating a sustainable building, one with zero net greenhouse emissions, the Nottinghamshire Wildlife Trust's Attenborough Nature Centre was designed and constructed with a great deal of thought and ingenuity (see online resources for a photograph of the Attenborough Nature Centre). The construction materials and methods used and the eco-friendly design mean that the centre demonstrates how, by using a range of specific features and technologies, a building can be constructed and run with the minimum of environmental impact.

Activities

Ⓔ Create a list

Ask the pupils to make a list of the environmentally-friendly things that they do in their home and/or school. This might include recycling glass, plastic and paper.

Ⓜ Recycling

Ask the pupils: What do you think is the value of recycling once used containers? How can this be seen as being 'green'? They should make a note of their ideas.

Ⓒ Green buildings

The Attenborough Nature Centre belongs to the Nottinghamshire Wildlife Trust. Ask the pupils: Why do you think it is particularly important for this organisation to have 'green building'?

Extension

Pupils should be directed to the photograph of the Attenborough Nature Reserve Visitors' Centre, found in the online resources. Draw their attention to the key 'green' features listed below. Pupils could then, singly or an a group, construct a diagram of the centre annotated to show the location of each of these features.

- High levels of insulation in the walls and the roof.

- Electricity for the centre is made by an array of south-facing photovoltaic cells.

- A 'heat pump' in the lake provides hot water for heating the building.

- Roof-mounted hot water solar panels.

- Storage space for recyclable waste materials.

- Windows designed to maximise use of natural light and solar heat so cutting down on lighting and heating needs.

The white-tailed eagle

Main topic: The economic advantages that can be gained from interventions and deliberate and scientifically-informed management of certain aspects of the environment.

Additional topic: The need for conservationists to convince people of the value of the reintroduction of birds and other animals to areas in which they once lived.

Key geographical questions:

• Who benefits from the reintroduction and re-establishment of iconic species of birds into areas of the countryside where they once lived?

• Why do some people perceive the reintroduction of birds of prey as a threat to their livelihood?

Online resources: White-tailed eagle information sheet; printable pupil stimulus material.

This could be used in conjunction with any topic that is looking at man's relationship with the environment. This work begins the examination of the benefits to tourism of the re-introduction of the white-tailed eagle, as seen in Mull, Skye and Wester Ross, balanced with the tensions between the stakeholders in the extension of the project into Fyfe in the east of Scotland.

Starter

Pupil stimulus

Provide pupils with the information sheet 'White-tailed eagle' (download from the online resources) which describes the white-tailed sea eagle, its history and impact on some local economies in Scotland.

Activities
❸ The question of reintroduction

It is quite often the activities of man that have made many animals and birds extinct. With a learning partner, ask the pupils to note down three reasons why we should reintroduce such animals and birds.

Ⓜ So what are the benefits?

Some of the people of Mull have benefitted greatly from the presence of the white-tailed eagles and other birds and animals that live on their island. With a learning partner, ask the pupils to note down as many ways that they can think of in which the island's economy benefits.

Ⓒ Comparing two ideas

The project to reintroduce the white-tailed eagle to Scotland began in the 1970s. At the same time, people were discussing the possibilities of reintroducing the wolf to Scotland as well. With a learning partner, ask the pupils to draw a table like the one below and put into it as many reasons for and against the reintroduction of the white-tailed eagle and the wolf you can think of.

	For	Against
White-tailed eagle		
Wolf		

Teacher's tips

- This group of tasks offers the opportunity to discuss the fact that reintroductions of predator species such as the eagle are often fraught with difficulty and set farmers, who see these initiatives as being potentially damaging to their livelihood, against such bodies as the RSPB. Scientific research, carried out on Mull in 1999 to assess the actual impact on the lambs of eagle predation, found that the loss of lambs to the resident eagles was minimal and posed no threat to the well-being of the flocks as a whole.

- Other reintroductions are planned, or are already taking place, in accordance with the European Commission Habitats Directive; the red kite (mid Wales, the Chilterns and various other areas), the great bustard (Salisbury Plain), the common crane (Somerset), the wild boar (the Forest of Dean), the beaver (Knapsdale in Scotland), a species of bumble bee and the pool frog. It would be valuable to look at these species and see how the reactions to them varied across the group.

Plenary

Pupil stimulus

Provide pupils with the information below before asking them to complete the activities.

Persecution in Fyfe?

In June 2013 it was reported that a tree had been cut down in a wood on a country estate in Fyfe in the east of Scotland. This is unremarkable except for the fact that in the tree was a nest currently being built by a pair of white-tailed eagles. Because of the protected status of the eagle the destruction of its nest is a criminal act, consequently this incident is the subject of an on-going investigation by the Scottish police force. The management of the estate has strenuously denied any involvement in the destruction of the tree and the nest.

Activities
❺ The legal protection of endangered species

Ask the pupils: Do you think it is right that birds of prey should be protected by law?

ⓜ Criminal acts of destruction

The incident described in the box above is a real event and it was reported in newspapers at the time. Ask the pupils: What do you think was the reason behind chopping down this particular tree? When people have been found guilty of this sort of offence in a court, what do you think should be their punishment?

ⓖ Human interventions

Ask the pupils to discuss with their learning partner what they think the arguments are (for and against) direct human intervention in the natural environment as we try to make it better after the activities of earlier generations have had such a damaging effect on certain areas.

Extension

Farmers find it hard enough to make a living as it is. Ask the pupils: What should organisations like the RSPB do to help the farmers to understand that they need not see the reintroduced species as a threat? Could there be financial help in the case of lambs being taken by eagles? How would it be possible to convince someone that reintroducing beavers or other large mammals, such as wolves, would be a good idea?

Living with conservation

Main topic: The development of sanctuaries for high status animals in the context of cultural understanding and diversity.

Key geographical questions:

- How important is it that we learn to live alongside the animals with whom we share the planet?

- How can possible conflicts be resolved when conservation projects are established in areas of high density human population?

Online resources: Printable pupil stimulus material.

The debate about the human needs of the millions of people whose lives are closely linked to the river Ganges in India is one of scale as much as complexity. Amidst the teeming humanity there lives a population of river dolphins that have gained protected and official National Aquatic Animal status. The pupil stimulus section below provides the information needed for pupils to discuss the issues and to examine the balance between the needs of the animals and the human stakeholders.

Starter

Pupil stimulus

The Vikramshila Gangetic Dolphin Sanctuary (VGDS)

The VGDS is in Bihar, a state in the north-east of India. It consists of a 65km long stretch of the Ganges River. The sanctuary was set up in 1991 because it was realised that if something wasn't done the Gangetic River Dolphin, already fully protected since 1972, would become extinct – just like its cousin the Yangtze River Dolphin in China.

Poverty
Along this stretch of the Ganges it is estimated that there are 3,000 families whose main source of livelihood is fishing – for their own consumption and for sale in local markets. As this is one of the world's most impoverished areas, schooling is scant as the efforts of all members are needed to contribute to the family income.

What is needed?

In order for the sanctuary to continue to work for everyone there are some important things that need to be in place. Conservation of this animal will only succeed when the river's resources are no longer over exploited.

Points for consideration

a) At the moment there is competition for the available fish between the dolphins and the people; fish stocks are reducing and the fish caught are smaller.

b) Dolphins must be protected against those who want to kill them for their meat and their oil.

c) The waters of this stretch of the Ganges are badly polluted by raw sewage, industrial and agricultural run-off.

d) Powered boats on the river frequently collide with dolphins as they surface to breathe. These collisions frequently kill or maim dolphins.

e) There is a lot of engineering work going on here, bridges for communication, dams across the river for irrigation of crops and the production of electricity. This disrupts the water flow, breaks up the dolphin populations and causes them to congregate in small areas of deeper water.

f) There are areas where the habitat has been damaged and needs to be restored.

g) Dolphins are an indicator species – healthy dolphins show that the river is healthy.

h) The human population needs to be educated about the need to conserve the ecology as a whole as well as the dolphins in particular. They need to understand what they are being asked to do.

i) Some fishermen lose up to half their catch to gangsters who run protection rackets in the villages along the river. When the fishermen don't pay up they are executed.

Activities

Ⓔ What would you change?

Ask the pupils to look at the list of 'Points for consideration' in the box above (these can also be found in the online resources). Ask them to choose one of them and with a partner decide two or three things that they feel could be done to achieve the necessary change. They should make a note of these to share with others in the class.

Ⓜ Priorities

All the points above are important in their own way. Ask the pupils to look at them carefully and decide in which order (from the most important downwards) they should be tackled. Ask them to make a note of this order to share with others in the class.

Ⓒ Plus – Minus – Interesting

Ask the pupils to look again at statement e) above. Rivers are dammed all over the world to provide vital power as well as helping to control seasonal flooding, allowing crops to be watered in a controlled way. Ask the pupils to divide a sheet of paper into three columns with headings Plus, Minus, Interesting. They should write statement e) across the top of the paper and then put down of all the ideas that they and their partner can think of and place them in the appropriate column:

- Plus column – the good things about the idea in statement e).

- Minus column – the bad things about the idea in statement e).

- Interesting column – the things that you find interesting about the idea in statement e).

Teacher's tips

- Two short videos (both under three minutes) that give an impression of the importance of this animal in India, atmospheric views of the river Ganges, some shots of the creature itself and a summary of some of the environmental issues can be found at:
  Video I http://www.youtube.com/watch?v=gdaqU203Zso
  Video 2 http://www.youtube.com/watch?v=gYGUfxE4Pto

- Groups could access these through tablet computers if available.

- The object of this stimulus is to get the pupils talking and discussing topics that they would not normally come across. They key idea is the interrelatedness of the components of the bigger picture. Ask the pupils to record their responses on large sticky notes and place these around the class for all to see.

- Good still pictures of the Gangetic River Dolphin – it is quite a distinctive species – can be found at: http://www.walkthroughindia.com/wildlife/dolphins-the-national-aquatic-animal-of-india/

- The PMI (Plus, Minus, Interesting) exercise is one of Edward de Bono's Cognitive Research Trust I approaches, the details of which can be found at: http://www.is-toolkit.com/workshop/pmi/BuildingVisionPMIModel.pdf

Plenary

Pupil stimulus

Ask the pupils to look again at Video 2 before completing the activities below. This gives an impression of the nature of the landscape of the Vikramshila Gangetic Dolphin Sanctuary as well as some shots of the creature itself.

Activities

❸ Looking at the landscape

Ask the pupils to write down three sentences that capture their immediate reaction to the landscape shown in this film.

ⓜ River features

The Ganges is one of the world's largest rivers – ask the pupils to write down three distinctive physical river features that they can see in this clip.

❻ What's the message?

Ask the pupils: Do you feel that the message of this advert comes over clearly? What message does it contain that you find interesting? What does it miss out?

Extension

Ask the pupils to take a minute to think about the features of their immediate environment (be it rural or urban or something in between). Ask them to think of the things they see as they travel to and from school. What needs changing and what would you change to make it better for humans, animals, wildlife?

Why 'dolphin–friendly' fishing?

Main topic: The interdependence of human livelihood and the needs of the environment.

Additional topic: Imaginative economic alternatives to fishing in Less Economically Developed Countries (LEDCs).

Key geographical questions:

- How do some fishing methods impact upon the welfare of the world's dolphins?

- What measures can be taken to reduce this impact?

Online resources: Printable pupil stimulus material.

This could be a useful contribution to work stimulating discussion about aspects of cultural understanding and diversity. The starter highlights the problem of by-catch and the plenary focuses on the practice of encouraging some fishing communities on the south coast of Zanzibar to alter age old practices, diversifying economic activity to the benefit of both themselves and the indigenous dolphin population.

Starter

Pupil stimulus

Provide pupils with the following information before asking them to complete the activities below.

Dolphins at risk

In the warm waters of the western Indian Ocean, near the island of Zanzibar, there live small populations of Indo-Pacific Humpback and Bottle-nose Dolphins. Both these species are endangered and although in 1996 an international agreement prohibited people from hunting them, their numbers are still very low and they are still suffering from man's fishing activity in the area.

Problem

Observers have discovered that 5.6% of the humpbacks and 8% of the bottle-noses are being killed each year because they get caught up in gill-nets. This is the kind of equipment used by the fishermen who catch their fish off the south coast of Zanzibar.

Gill-nets

These are large fishing nets, like enormous long curtains. They sit vertically in the water because they have floats attached to the top and weights attached to the bottom. Fish cannot see these nets and as they swim into them they become entangled in the mesh by their gills. The dolphins can't see these nets and their echo location doesn't pick them up either so they approach the fish caught there, thinking that there is a tasty snack, and they too get caught up in the mesh. When they can't return to the surface to breathe, they drown.

Activities

ⓔ Animal welfare

Ask the pupils: Why is it important that we consider the welfare of marine creatures such as whales and dolphins?

ⓜ Human impact

Ask the pupils: What would be the impact on the people of the south coast of Zanzibar if they were forced to catch less fish?

ⓒ The importance of fishing

Ask the pupils to discuss and write down two or three reasons why they think fishing is so important to the people of Zanzibar.

Teacher's tip

It would be useful for the pupils to be familiar with the location of Zanzibar, the principles of gill-netting and the concept of by-catch, which is when non-targeted animals are inadvertently caught by gill-netting and other fishing techniques. This is a major issue worldwide, with an estimated 300,000 plus cetaceans of all kinds being killed each year as a direct result of entrapment and entanglement in a variety of forms of widely-used fishing gear. It would also be valuable for the pupils to be familiar with the term ecotourism.

Plenary

Pupil stimulus

Provide the pupils with the information below before asking them to complete the following activities.

Ecotourism – could this be a solution?

Abasi and Haji are brothers; they live in Kizimkazi, a village on the south coast of Zanzibar, an island in the Indian Ocean off the coast of Tanzania. They are fishermen by trade; they know about fishing, about boats and about the sea. They used to go hunting for the dolphins; they used the flesh as bait for other forms of fishing. But now they have a new job. They still hunt dolphins, but not in order to kill them, they hunt them now so that they can show them to the tourists that come from all over the world to visit Zanzibar. The two brothers are using their skills and experience to help preserve the dolphins by taking people to see them up close and personal and thereby enabling more and more people to realise what amazing creatures they are. This is a new way of making a living.

Activities

🄴 Using skills

Ask the pupils to describe how they imagine the skills of the fishermen Abasi and Haji will be used in their new jobs as guides for ecotourists.

🄼 Impact of work

Ask the pupils: What do you think will be the impact of the brothers' new jobs on their families?

🄲 Looking at the effects

Ask the pupils: What effects do you imagine this sort of idea will have on the economy of the island? Are these effects going to be all beneficial? Can you see problems that might arise?

Extension

Ecotourism is an important part of the economy of many LEDCs. Many people from wealthier countries are keen to travel across the globe to see breathtaking landscapes and beautiful animals, plants and birds that they can't see at home. Often this has the effect of focusing efforts to conserve endangered habitats and threatened species.

Ask the pupils to think of three benefits and three drawbacks that might be associated with developing ecotourism on a tropical island such as Zanzibar.

Section 8

Major challenges in the UK today

The effects of the weather on different UK traders

Main topic: The influence of the weather on people's livelihoods.

Additional topic: Global warming and its effects on people.

Key geographical questions:

- How can the weather affect the profits of various street traders in the UK?

- Could climate change force certain street traders to permanently change their operations?

This starter and plenary provides an ideal primer for any unit of work on the weather, providing a tangible link to the lives of real people and requiring pupils to consider the economic implications of different types of weather – both locally and further afield.

Starter

Pupil stimulus

Over the last few years the weather in the UK has been extremely variable. We have experienced record amounts of snow in late winter, torrential downpours leading to floods in spring and extended summer heatwaves during the school holidays. Market-stall holders, ice-cream vendors and *Big Issue* sellers are just some of the many people whose livelihoods are affected by the changing weather. Many scientists believe that the erratic weather that has affected the UK recently is a consequence of global warming and the erratic patterns are set to become more common. This has serious implications for many traders who are vulnerable to weather changes.

Activities
❶ Types of traders

With a learning partner, ask the pupils to identify a type of trader whose business is affected by the weather and explain how they are affected.

Ⓜ Impact of the weather

Ask the pupils: What could a specific trader do to reduce the impact the weather has on their business?

Ⓒ Adapting to change

Ask the pupils to prepare a list of bullet points to be read out at a local Chamber of Trade meeting to help traders understand how their operations will have to adapt if global warming continues to make our weather so variable.

Teacher's tips

- Make sure your pupils know the difference between *weather* and *climate*, and the types of words that are used to describe each.

- It will help your pupils if you can take them on an imaginary tour of their local town/ village centre etc. to remind them of the range of traders who work there (you could use Google StreetView to show them actual images of nearby settlements).

- The emphasis in this entry is on *smaller* traders, especially those who conduct their operations on the street, though the weather clearly also affects larger traders too.

Plenary

Pupil stimulus

The following types of trader are often affected by changes in the weather:

- a market-stall holder selling coats, hats and umbrellas

- an ice-cream seller (visiting residential streets in his or her van)

- a *Big Issue* seller.

Activities

Ⓔ Which weather?

Ask the pupils to choose one of the above three traders and with a learning partner identify a type of weather that would help them sell *more* of their goods. They should then identify a type of weather that would result in them selling less of their goods. In each case they should explain why.

Ⓜ Daily forecasts

Ask the pupils: Which of the traders would be able to make best use of detailed daily forecasts provided a week ahead, in order to plan where and when they should head out in search of custom? They should explain how they would make use of the forecasts.

Ⓒ Local businesses

Ask the pupils to imagine they run a weather forecast services company and are considering approaching business in your local area to offer some new services specifically for them. Ask them to draw up a shortlist of the five to ten businesses that they would approach first and explain how their weather services could help each of them.

> ### Teacher's tips
>
> - Pupils would probably find it helpful if you did a thought-showering exercise to document the various types of stalls commonly found on markets, before they attempted the above activities.
>
> - Try to make the most of any pupils with experience of working on market stalls, as it is a fairly common Saturday job for older teenagers.

Extension

Change the scale of this topic by considering the effects of the weather on large businesses. Due to the range of goods they sell, supermarkets are an excellent example of a business that is affected by the weather on a monthly or even weekly basis. Ask your pupils to prepare a month-by-month chart showing how the sales of different goods in supermarkets can be affected by weather changes over the course of a year. You could also ask them to annotate their chart with details of the main people in the business that will have to carry out actions in response to the weather changes, and what these actions might be.

Seeking new opportunities in the UK

Main topic: Migration and the reasons people move from one country to another.

Additional topic: The effect of global inequalities on different countries.

Key geographical questions:

- Why do people travel long distances to start a new life in the UK?

- Do they find what they are expecting when they arrive?

Online resources: Personal account from three people who have moved to the UK; printable pupil stimulus materials.

This is an ideal activity with which to begin a unit of work on migration or global inequality more generally. It helps pupils get a real sense of the issues affecting people in other countries on a day to day basis, and how these can lead to migration to countries such as the UK.

Starter

Pupil stimulus

Show students the pupil stimulus material below, as well as the personal accounts that can be found online, explaining why three people from Poland, Somalia and Kurdistan came to live in the UK.

Migration to the UK

For people wanting to escape poverty or other major difficulties in their own countries, the UK has been seen as a 'land of new opportunities' for many decades. Large-scale immigration into the country began in the 1950s, shortly after World War Two ended, when the UK was trying to re-build its manufacturing industries to boost an economy that had been battered by war. At this time tens of thousands of people from British Commonwealth countries in the Caribbean (especially Jamaica) and India were invited to the UK to work in factories. Many of these people stayed on in the country and helped to build the multicultural society that the UK is today.

More recently, the UK has provided a safe refuge for people escaping war and persecution in countries such as Iraq, Somalia and Syria. Many of these people have applied for 'asylum', which gives them the right to live and work in the UK. However, some of these people have found it difficult to find work in the UK, mostly because they lack the necessary job skills or do not speak English very well.

The latest major migration has seen people from poorer European countries such as Poland and the Czech Republic, which have recently become part of the European Union, travel to Britain. They have mainly sought jobs in service industries – for example in bars, hotels and restaurants. It is estimated that at least 500,000 new migrants from Eastern Europe have arrived in the UK in the last five years.

Activities

Ⓔ Improvements

Ask the pupils to choose one of the stories featured and with a learning partner make a note of all the ways in which the person's life improved by moving to the UK.

Ⓜ Difficulties

Ask the pupils to study the three stories and identify any ways in which life in the UK could be difficult for the people mentioned.

Ⓒ Why move to the UK?

Despite the difficulties and dangers of moving to the UK, many tens thousands of people continue to try to do so. Ask the pupils to work with a learning partner to identify the reasons they continue to do this, and prepare their answer as an illustrated PowerPoint slide or two.

Teacher's tip

It is important for pupils to listen to the detail of the above stories rather than be unduly influenced by what they see reported in the newspapers, or hear their parents/carers say. Encourage them to be discerning in their treatment of source material.

Plenary

Activities

🅔 Problems for migrants

Ask the pupils to make a list of some of the problems that migrants experience when they arrive in a new country.

🅜 Reducing the numbers

Ask the pupils to work with a learning partner to identify five things that need to change in order to reduce the number of people who want to move to the UK.

🅒 The economy and lives

Ask the pupils to write the script of a short news report showing the range of ways in which migrants can help improve the economy and enhance the quality of life for people in the UK.

Teacher's tip

This is clearly a topic with the potential to be controversial, not least because there are likely to be at least some recent immigrants living in your community – including immigrant children attending your school. You should try to help your pupils understand that one of the roles of geographers is to look carefully at the available information on social issues and offer practical solutions that help people to live better lives.

Extension

Bring this topic to life for your pupils by arranging for somebody who has recently settled in the UK to come and speak to the class. This will create a powerful sense of immediacy and authenticity, and allow your pupils to ask questions that will enable them to make a personal connection to a real person affected by the issues highlighted in this entry.

Managing our dwindling energy supplies

Main topic: The development of an understanding of the need to increase and develop renewable energy sources to help to address the issues of global climate change.

Additional topic: The possible impacts on communities of the use of land-based wind farms.

Key geographical questions:

- How can local communities use renewable resource technology to make meaningful contributions in the battle to reduce carbon emissions?

- How would this impact on the energy use of individuals and communities?

Online resources: Pupil stimulus material.

This group of ideas provides an opportunity to start, to deepen or to widen discussions on the generating of green energy using wind power in the context of the broader discussion about climate change and the impact of human activity upon this.

Starter

Pupil stimulus

Wind power – a renewable resource

Wind power is a green, renewable source of energy that can be harnessed to produce electricity. The advantage that wind power has over other methods of generating much-needed electricity is that it does not burn fossil fuel; the generating of power in this way does not contribute to carbon emissions.

To harness wind power we need a turbine that is driven round by the wind. This is connected to a generator and the power produced can then be used immediately or stored in a battery.

Small scale

The essential process is quite simple and small scale wind-powered generating systems can be bought for as little as £500. Some turbines are small enough to be fixed on to a caravan and can power the fridge, lights and the television. Larger turbines can be used to provide the energy for a farm, a small factory or a school; still larger ones could provide enough power for all the houses in a village. Then, at the top of the scale, there are the large turbines arranged in wind farms built by the large energy companies that generate a significant proportion of the nation's energy needs. These are situated in areas where the wind can be relied upon, off-shore around the coast and also in hilly rural areas.

Activities

🅔 Your neighbourhood

Ask the pupils to imagine a plan has been put forward to site a wind turbine near to where they live. What would their feelings be about this? Ask them to note down three good points and three bad points of this plan from their point of view.

🅜 Where is the problem?

Ask the pupils: What do you think are the objections to the siting of wind turbines? Ask them to make a note of the problems that might be faced by:

• local residents

• farmers in the area

• local businesses.

🅒 Wind turbine for the school

Explain to the pupils that your school has been given a grant to build a wind turbine capable of generating up to 75% of the school's energy needs. Do they think this is this a good use of money? Where should the turbine be sited?

Teacher's tip

There is a wide variety of material available online that will help to broaden the pupils' understanding of renewable sources of energy:

• wind power: http://www.renewableuk.com

• renewables in general: http://www.cat.org.uk/

• good accessible technical information: http://www.darvill.clara.net/altenerg/wind.htm

Plenary

Pupil stimulus

Using less energy

The essential message here is that we need to use less energy. But how can we do this? This is an issue that everyone needs to think about carefully, from the government down to each individual member of society. Our lives are full of energy-consuming devices, some we find essential to our way of life, some we could perhaps use less or not use at all.

Activities

E Could you use less energy?

Ask the pupils to make a list of all the electric appliances that you personally use in your home. Ask them to give each one a rating from one (essential) to five (not very important) according to how important that piece of equipment is to the home.

M Using less energy in the home

Ask the pupils to look at this list:

• insulation in the walls

• insulation in the roof space

• using long-life light bulbs

• turning off lights when not in use

• not leaving the TV on stand-by.

With a learning partner they should discuss these energy-saving methods and decide on an effectiveness score from one (the most effective) to five (the least effective).

C Using less energy in school

Ask the pupils: How do you think you could save energy in your school? What would your plan to save energy look like? On one side of paper (only) ask them to draft your school energy-saving plan.

Extension

Other renewable sources of energy are available, for example:

- solar power

- wave power

- hydro-electric power

- biogas (a mixture of methane and CO_2 formed by decomposing organic matter)

- tidal barrages.

Working with a partner or alone, ask the pupils to choose two of these and quickly put down their instinctive reactions – the positives and the negatives. Share their ideas.

The environmental performance of fast-food outlets

Main topic: The impact of the fast-food sector on the environment.

Additional topic: How major companies can reduce their impact on the environment.

Key geographical questions:

• How environmentally-friendly are fast-food stores?

• To what extent is it possible for fast-food stores to be environmentally friendly in every way?

Online resources: Subway leaflet.

These activities are best used towards the end of a unit of work on the retail or service sector. They could also be slotted into a series of lessons looking at how the environment is affected by various kinds of industries.

Starter

Pupil stimulus

The major fast-food companies in the UK have come under a lot of pressure from environmental groups to reduce their impact on the environment – in particular that caused by the production of the food they serve and by the waste that is produced through their operations. For this activity the pupils are going to look at a leaflet produced by the 'design-your-own' sandwich store Subway, whose motto is 'eat fresh'. The leaflet (which you can find in the online resources) explains how as a company Subway is trying to keep the planet as healthy as possible in order to meet its commitment to become more environmentally responsible.

Activities
❺ Marks out of ten

Ask the pupils to make a list of all the ways in which Subway is trying to reduce its impact on the environment. They should then give the company a score out of ten for how well they think it is doing to meet its commitment to become more environmentally responsible (where ten = extremely well).

Ⓜ The most positive impact

Ask the pupils: Which of the measures outlined in the leaflet will have the most positive impact on the environment? Ask them to swap their answer with a learning partner and justify it.

Ⓒ Five additional measures

Working in a group of four, ask the pupils to prepare a list of at least five additional measures that Subway could take to reduce its impact on the environment still further.

Teacher's tips

- The business operations of major fast-food chains such as Subway, McDonald's and KFC are huge and highly complex and there are very many ways in which the environment can be affected. Encourage pupils to consider these diverse effects and look beyond the immediate impacts that are obvious when visiting the stores.

- It is possible that some of your pupils (or their siblings) may have part-time jobs in a local Subway store, or another fast-food outlet. This could lead to sensitivities if the classroom mood becomes overcritical of such businesses, which clearly serve a need whether or not you visit them.

- It is also important not to take the stance that all fast-food outlets are bad and deserve heavy criticism for their poor environmental performance. Such stores provide valuable employment opportunities and often score highly in worker-satisfaction surveys, as well as making important contributions to local and national community groups and charities.

Plenary

Pupil stimulus

This activity challenges the pupils to imagine they are trying to set up the UK's most environmentally-friendly fast-food outlet in their local settlement.

Activities

Ⓔ Justify the claim

Working in groups of four, ask the pupils to make a list of at least ten different areas that they will need tackle in order to justify the claim that their fast-food outlet is the most environmentally-friendly one in the UK.

Ⓜ Easy and difficult changes

Some aspects of the pupils' operation will be difficult to make environmentally friendly, while for others the process will be straightforward. Ask them to draw a two-columned table and in it list five aspects of their business that will be *easy* to make environmentally friendly and five that will be more *difficult*.

Ⓒ Barriers to the goal

Ask the pupils: To what extent is it possible to run a fast-food outlet that is also very friendly to the environment? What are the main barriers that make such a goal difficult?

Teacher's tips

- You may wish to provide a visual prompt to help pupils consider the full range of environmental impacts caused by fast-food outlets (e.g. a mind-map, photo-montage or series of icons).

- Exploit the knowledge of any pupils in your class with experience of working in fast-food outlets. It is empowering for pupils to share their knowledge with their classmates in this way.

Extension

This work should stimulate pupils' interest in the environmental credentials of other fast-food outlets in your local town and further afield. It would be interesting for pupils to carry out some further research into the UK's major fast-food companies and, using an objective scoring system, try to ascertain which company appears to have the best environmental credentials. Such companies invest heavily in their customer service departments and they should be very accommodating of any pupil requests for further information.

How could you improve quality of life in Britain?

Main topic: Quality of life in the UK.

Additional topic: How governments can affect quality of life through the work of Parliament.

Key geographical questions:

- How can quality of life be improved in Britain?

- What are the priorities in trying to improve quality of life in Britain?

Online resources: Printable pupil stimulus material.

This starter/plenary can be used as a prelude to any topic that considers quality of life or inequality issues. It is designed to engage pupils by asking them to place themselves in a decision-making role; it also helps them to see the complexities involved in tackling quality of life issues and how actions often need to be prioritised.

Starter

Pupil stimulus

Could you change the country for the better?

The role of the British government is to try to make the country a better place in which to live and work. It does this by managing the country's finances carefully and introducing policies that will increase prosperity, improve health care and education, and enhance the environment. Every four or five years the general public gets the chance to elect a new government when they vote in a *general election* – the political party that has the largest number of Members of Parliament (MPs) elected gets to form the government. In order to make major changes to the key systems affecting the country, the elected government – or any individual Members of Parliament – can put forward draft laws called *Bills*. These are presented to parliament and MPs vote to establish whether they become laws.

Activities

ⓔ Problems to tackle

Ask the pupils to identify five problems in the UK today that the government should tackle, which would improve quality of life for most people.

ⓜ Devise a law

Ask the pupils to work with a learning partner to devise one law that would make a significant difference to quality of life in the UK.

ⓒ Spend wisely

Ask the pupils to imagine they had one billion pounds (that's £1,000 million) to spend on new measures to improve quality of life in the UK. What laws would need to be introduced to make sure the money is spent sensibly and fairly? How would they help?

Teacher's tip

This is an opportunity for your pupils to do some free, creative thinking on the broad subject of improving the quality of life. They may have little idea how parliament and the government works, so this may need to be explained carefully to them, perhaps using a video clip taken during a parliamentary debate (there are plenty on YouTube).

Plenary

Activities

ⓔ Governments

Working with a learning partner, ask the pupils to make a list of five reasons why it is difficult for governments to improve quality of life for all members of the community.

ⓜ Health, education or leisure?

Ask the pupils: If a government had to choose between only spending money on health, education or leisure activities, which should take priority and why?

ⓒ The role of people

Some think that people, as well as the government, have a role in improving their own quality of life. Ask the pupils to what extent they think this true in the UK? Are things different in poorer countries? Explain that they must justify their answers.

Teacher's tip

It would be interesting for your pupils to hear the views of your Member of Parliament or a local councillor on the above issues. Such a person may be able to send you a written statement to read out in class, or might even consider visiting your pupils for a question and answer session.

Extension

A natural follow-up to this topic would be to study the passage of a Bill through parliament and on to the statute book, that is set to have an impact on quality of life in the UK. An opportunity to study the complexities of the law-making system and the work of the British Parliament will be invaluable in opening up the process of high level decision-making to your pupils.

Section 9

Sustainable development in the 21st century

Aquaculture – do the costs outweigh the benefits?

Main topic: In the drive to produce food for the expanding world population the rapid growth of aquaculture poses serious risks to both the environment and the wild stocks of ocean fish.

Key geographical questions:

- What are the main benefits of the worldwide growth in aquaculture?

- What are the costs to the environment? Do they outweigh the benefits?

Online resources: Printable pupil stimulus material; environmental impact of aquaculture information sheet.

This topic could be used as an example of the expansion of a practice that was originally seen to be beneficial to the environment, to the point where it is now seen in quite another light.

Starter

Pupil stimulus

A multi-billion pound global industry

Aquaculture is a primary industry and is critically important in the production of high quality food the world over. Fish farming across the word has grown incredibly – probably by as much as eight per cent per year since the 1960s. Figures published by the Food and Agriculture Organisation of the United Nations show that fish farms produced nearly 47% of the 128 million tonnes of fish consumed by the world's population in 2010.

Aquaculture
Fish farming is now a multi-billion pound global industry employing an estimated 55 million people – between 10% and 12% of the world's population gain their livelihood from aquaculture. Much of this employment is on small fish farms supplying food to the local area through local markets, but some fish farms are constructed and managed on an industrial scale and the fish, shell fish and crustaceans produced by these farms are distributed around the globe.

Activities

Show the pupils the information sheet 'Environmental impact of aquaculture' (download from the online resources) before asking them to complete one or more of the following activities.

ⓔ Good impact and bad impact

Tell the pupils to make two columns on a page, one headed 'good impacts', the other 'bad impacts', then ask them to decide for each of the statements on the information sheet whether they go in the good column or the bad column and to write the letter of the statement in the appropriate column.

ⓜ On a scale of 1 to 5

Ask the pupils to look carefully at each of the statements. They should discuss them with a learning partner and score each one out of five – where one is very damaging and five is very beneficial. Next ask them to put them in rank order. Ask the pupils: What does this tell you about the solutions to problems such as this?

ⓒ A question of balance

From the statements in the box, ask the pupils to choose a high impact 'good' statement and a high impact 'bad' statement. With a partner, ask them to discuss and note down the implications carried by each of these statements as they understand them. Ask: What would your solution be to the issue mentioned on your chosen 'bad' impact statement? Would that solution have an influence on your chosen 'good' impact?

Teacher's tips

- Pollution is the major local problem associated with aquaculture with wide and serious impacts on the environment, particularly in the case of 'open' systems sited in rivers or off-shore. Pollutants are typically: fish faeces, waste food, pharmaceuticals (from the medication of the fish) and the anti-fouling agents used on the cages (butyltins). The seabed beneath the fish farm is frequently choked with a poisonous cocktail of chemical and decaying matter.

- Print off and create card-sort sets of the statements so that the pupils can handle them and physically move them around as they discuss the content of each. This would be appropriate for all the tasks.

- Web links to WWF and to the United Nations material:
  http://wwf.panda.org/what_we_do/endangered_species/cetaceans/threats/fish_farms/
  http://www.fao.org/docrep/016/i2727e/i2727e00.htm

Plenary

Pupil stimulus

The Argyle and Bute Council has received an application to establish a salmon farm on dry land. The plan involves building a warehouse on a disused airfield in which the tanks of fish will be housed. Other features of the planned farm are:

- It will be a closed system and the water it uses will be recycled on site.

- Because of this there will be no sea lice that trouble other salmon farms.

- Therefore no chemicals will have to be used to control them.

- The power to run the farm will be from solar panels.

- The food given to the fish (rag-worms) will be bred on the site.

Activities

ⓔ Great new venture

Ask the pupils: Would you give this scheme the go-ahead? Ask them to discuss their answer to this with a partner, giving the reasons for your decision.

ⓜ Great for the environment

This scheme seems to have thought of everything – ask the pupils if they can think of other issues that they might want to discuss with the company.

ⓒ But will it work?

Ask the pupils to look carefully at the issues raised in the starter section. Does this plan raise any other questions that they would want to ask the company? What other reassurances would they need to be certain that the company's carbon footprint was as small as possible and that it had covered all the ecological bases?

Extension

The problems discussed in this chapter are to do with feeding an ever-growing world population without destroying the very planet on which this food has to be grown. Ask the pupils: What policies would you like to see world leaders put in to place to avert disaster?

Fairtrade farming – producing cocoa in Ghana

Main topic: Understanding the interactions between places and the networks created by flows of information, people and goods.

Additional topic: Understanding the value to the well-being of people that comes from the adoption of ethical ways of carrying out intercontinental trade.

Key geographical questions:

* What are the principles behind the Fairtrade movement and how do the cocoa farmers of Ghana benefit?

* How can our buying decisions in the UK impact on the quality of life of people thousands of miles away?

Online resources: Printable pupil stimulus material; Fairtrade Principles factsheet; worksheets.

This series of tasks could begin, or help to continue, discussions about the concept of fair trade. By looking at a familiar world commodity in the context of the ethics of its production, marketing and end use we can explore some of the levels of interrelatedness that need to be understood as pupils gain a geographical imagination and an understanding of the workings of important aspects of the world economy.

Starter

Pupil stimulus

Unfair trade

In the world there are millions of people who work long hours and use the skills and experience of generations to produce crops that are highly valued on the world market. However, the marketing, transport and processing of many of these crops is in the hands of large companies. These companies use their power to ensure that the growers get only a fraction of what the crop is worth and so they and their families live in or around the poverty level and never benefit from the value to the world of their efforts. This situation impoverishes the people themselves and also the communities in which they live.

Fairtrade

Fairtrade was set up in the late 1980s and exists to give disadvantaged farmers and farm workers across the world a better deal. The Fairtrade Foundation was started in 1992 and the vision of the organisation as stated on their website is:

'... of a world in which justice and sustainable development are at the heart of trade structures and practices so that everyone, through their work, can maintain a decent and dignified livelihood and develop their full potential.'

(http://www.fairtrade.org.uk/what_is_fairtrade/fairtrade_foundation.aspx)

Community benefits

The development of fair trading systems enables growers to work together to get fair prices for their crops. They can then maintain and develop their communities and ensure that there is access to schooling, healthcare, improved electricity and water supply, sanitation and good communications systems (road, rail and electronic). Fairtrade arrangements mean that farmers can invest in their farms and continue to develop and improve their crops and produce them efficiently.

Many different crops

Fairtrade agreements have been made across the world with producers of such things as: coffee, tea, sugar, cocoa (for chocolate), cotton, pineapples, bananas, fruit for juices, dried fruit, cereals and honey.

Many different products

There are now about 130 products on the supermarket shelves that are manufactured with Fairtrade ingredients including beers, wines, cakes, biscuits, beauty products, ice cream, and jam. You can even now buy jewellery made from Fairtrade gold!

Provide pupils with the online 'Fact sheet' – 'Fairtrade farming – producing cocoa in Ghana' (see online resources) to enable them to find the information needed for the tasks.

Follow the link to the short film 'Swap your choc', a film about Kuap Kokoo at:

http://www.fairtrade.org.uk/resources/films/cocoa_swap_your_choc.aspx

Activities

❷ Human impact

Ask the pupils: How many Fairtrade products can you list that you have seen in your local supermarket? How many have you have used at home? Ask them to check the Fairtrade website to remind themselves of the distinctive logo that they use to mark the packets of their goods.

Ⓜ Community impact

In small groups, ask the pupils to look at the information in the Fairtrade Premium section of the 'act sheet' online. Discuss the impact of each and then rank each of these effects of the premium in order of importance to the quality of life in the village communities. Encourage them to use the online 'Table 1' to help organise their thoughts.

Ⓒ Consumer impact

The origins of the Fairtrade movement lie in the uncomfortable realisation that many farmers throughout the world are not getting a fair deal. Ask the pupils: How could you convince your family that using Fairtrade products was ethical? This could be carried out as an individual task, but would probably be better done in a group of three or four.

Teacher's tips

- The Fairtrade website is an excellent resource for these tasks. You could begin with the short film at: http://www.fairtrade.org.uk/resources/films/cocoa_swap_your_choc. aspx

- This can be downloaded free and provides some very useful background to the specific issues under discussion.

- The 'Fact sheet' (see online resources) has been designed to complement the film clip and provide the jumping off points for both the Starter and the Plenary tasks.

Plenary

Pupil stimulus

Revisit the film 'Swap your choc' looking carefully at the subtitles.

Activities

Ⓔ Working with cocoa

The images in the film are very striking. Ask the pupils: What are the key things that you notice about how the people work with the cocoa pods and the cocoa beans? What would explain this?

Ⓜ Changing lives

In small groups, ask the pupils to agree on the four most important effects that the Fairtrade organisation has had on the lives of the people in the film. Ask them to give each idea a number from one to four to show the order of importance.

Ⓖ Making changes to society

Ask the pupils to look at the Fairtrade Principles on the 'Fact sheet'. They should then complete 'Table 2' (see online resources) in which they say what they think might be the positive changes that these could make to Ghanaian rural society.

Extension

Ask the pupils to look at the 'Kuapa Kokoo and Fairtrade' section of the website: http://www.fairtrade.org.uk/producers/cacao/kuapa_kokoo_union.aspx. With a partner they should draft a statement of no more than 50 words that encapsulates the benefits of this cooperative to the growers and its relationship with Fairtrade.

A car for everyone?

Main topic: Economic development and standard of living.

Additional topic: The car as a driver of social change.

Key geographical questions:

- What effects will the availability of a very cost-effective car have on the people of India?

- In what other ways can standard of living be judged in countries such as India?

These activities would be best used after pupils have studied the economy and standard of living in at least one Less Economically Developed Country.

Starter

Pupil stimulus

The world's cheapest car was launched in India for the staggeringly low price of £1,500. The Tata Nano is set to revolutionise transport for millions of Indians who, until now, could not afford a new reliable car to use for work or pleasure. The Tata Nano is very much a stripped-down vehicle which comes with only the very basic equipment. There are no airbags in the vehicle and a radio is not even provided as standard! But this allows the manufacturers to keep the cost down and it is expected that millions of Tata Nanos will be on the roads of India in a few years' time.

The Wikipedia page about the Tata Nano car is particularly informative and contains some interesting information on how Tata Motors have managed to strip the car back to keep costs down: http://en.wikipedia.org/wiki/Tata_Nano

Activities
❸ Quality of life

Ask the pupils: How could the launch of the Tata Nano car help to improve the quality of life of those Indians that can afford one?

Ⓜ Pros and cons

Ask the pupils to discuss with a learning partner the pros and cons of the extremely cheap Tata Nano car for the people of India. They should then make a note of the most significant points to come out of their discussion.

Ⓒ Problems

Ask the pupils: To what extent do you agree with the following statement? The launch of the Tata Nano car is likely to bring with it more problems than it solves for the country of India. Make sure they justify their answers.

Teacher's tips

- It is useful to put the launch of the Tata Nano car in the context of average household incomes in India to show that although it is cheap by Western standards, it is still well beyond the reach of most Indian families.

- Your pupils would also find it beneficial to understand the history of private car ownership in the UK, which only started to become widespread in the 1960s and 1970s as incomes rose in the post-World War Two era. The phenomenon of 'two-car families' is an even more recent development, that has only become commonplace in the last two decades. Despite these developments, in some disadvantaged parts of the UK – especially in the poorer areas of the major cities – car ownership is still far from universal.

Plenary

Pupil stimulus

Increasing levels of private car ownership are just one indicator of rising standards of living for people in poorer countries such as India. There are many other indicators that geographers use to determine that prosperity in these countries is increasing – at least for some sectors of society.

Activities

Ⓔ Standard of living

Ask the pupils to identify three other indicators of rising standard of living in poorer countries.

Ⓜ Health, education and leisure

Ask the pupils to work with a learning partner to identify two indicators of rising standard of living in poorer countries under each of the following headings: Health, Education, Leisure time.

Ⓒ Most important indicator

Ask the pupils: Of all the indicators of rising standard of living in poorer countries which indicator (or indicators) do you think are the *most* important and why?

Teacher's tips

• The statistics around such things as infant mortality, life expectancy and literacy in many poorer countries are likely to come as a shock to many of your pupils, and you should go through each of these carefully and explain their implications for young and older people.

• It is important that your pupils understand the great *diversity* of circumstances for different groups of people in both poor and richer countries. Just because a statistic may indicate that less children are dying as babies in the country, this does not mean that lower infant mortality is enjoyed equally by all members of the population.

Extension

Try to organise a geographically-themed assembly at least once every term in your school. The topics covered in this starter and plenary are highly suitable as assembly material. Given the appropriate support it is surprising how pupils can rise to the challenge of staging an assembly for their peers – especially if it deals with issues that they feel passionate about. Several charities produce excellent free support packs for assemblies dealing with contemporary social issues such as inequality, social justice etc. (for example see www.amnesty.org.uk or www.oxfam.org.uk).

Sustainable development of tropical forests

Main topic: Tropical forests and their conservation.

Additional topic: Economic development in the rural regions of poorer countries.

Key geographical questions:

- How can tropical forests bring benefits to local people?

- How can tropical forests be managed in a more sustainable way?

Online resources: Images of Reserva Utuana; interview with a local guide.

The following activities are best placed at the end of a teaching sequence on tropical forests or economic development in poorer countries.

Starter

Pupil stimulus

There has been a lot of interest over recent years in the conservation of the world's tropical forests, one of the most remarkable and important habitats on earth. As well as providing a home to millions of plant and animal species, tropical forests also provide a refuge for large numbers of indigenous *people* who live in small villages under the cover of the forest, in a manner unchanged for thousands of years. The tropical forests are also thought to play a significant role in regulating the world's climate by absorbing carbon dioxide from the atmosphere, thereby helping to prevent or slow down global warming.

One of the most difficult challenges in creating a sustainable future for the tropical forests is finding a way for forests to be protected, while also ensuring that the needs of a growing local population are met. In this case study the pupils will be looking at 'Reserva Utuana', a community nature reserve in the Andes of southern Ecuador, South America, where local people are living in harmony with wildlife. Show the pupils the images of Reserva Utuana from the online resources and the wildlife that lives there, and there is also an interview with Rodrigo, a local guide, to read.

Activities

ⓔ Benefits to the guide

Ask the pupils: What benefits does Rodrigo get from working at Reserva Utuana?

ⓜ Local involvement

Ask the pupils: Why does the involvement of local people in the running of Reserva Utuana make it more likely that the reserve will be a success?

ⓒ The main threats

Ask the pupils: What are the main threats to Reserva Utuana and what can be done to manage these threats?

Teacher's tips

- Although your pupils are likely to already be familiar with tropical rainforests from previous studies, there are actually many *different types* of tropical forest. The tropical forest within Reserva Utuana is montane in nature and is also known as 'cloud forest', as it is often draped in cloud.

- Your pupils would probably find some additional geographical context to the country of Ecuador useful, as it is less frequently studied than other South American countries. It is a fascinating and incredibly diverse country – little bigger in size than the UK – which has strong tourism and oil-extraction industries and is also where the Panama hat originated. The Galapagos Islands, made famous by Charles Darwin's expedition and theories, are also part of Ecuador.

Plenary

Pupil stimulus

Sustainable development is the process of developing an area in a careful way to ensure it lasts for a long time. Ask the pupils to re-read the interview with Rodrigo Espinosa, the wildlife guide at Reserva Utuana, and answer one of the questions below.

Activities

Ⓔ Sustainable?

Ask the pupils to make a list of the ways in which Reserva Utuana is being managed in a *sustainable* way.

ⓂLocal people

Ask the pupils: Why is it important for *local people* that Reserva Utuana is managed sustainably?

ⒸA good example

Ask the pupils: To what extent is Reserva Utuana a good example of sustainable development in action, that can serve as a blueprint for tropical forests elsewhere?

Teacher's tip

Your pupils would probably find it useful to have some further examples of projects that demonstrate the principles of sustainable development – especially those from Less Economically Developed Countries. Two particularly good examples are the growing of fair trade products such as bananas and coffee while also trying to maintain high levels of biodiversity, and the collection of forest products such as Brazil nuts in an environmentally sensitive way.

Extension

These activities would be the ideal springboard for further studies looking at how sustainable development can be applied to other aspects of managing tropical rainforests. There are, in particular, clear links with the following challenges: timber extraction, road building, extraction of forest products, extraction of raw materials, mining and agricultural expansion.

Section 10

Geographical reflection

Reflecting on your geography course

Main topic: Reflection on learning.

Key geographical question: Which parts of the course have you found most enjoyable over the last year and why?

This is a self-contained synoptic activity that can be carried out at the beginning or end of a lesson. It needs to be carried out as a term draws to a close, so pupils can look back on what they have learnt. It is designed to encourage pupils to reflect on their geographical learning over a term and consider the parts of the course they have most enjoyed. Note that this activity can be run either as a starter or a plenary within a lesson; unlike most of the entries in the book it is does not contain a separate starter and plenary with different activities, designed to be used in the same lesson.

Starter/plenary

Pupil stimulus

Before beginning the activity pupils should be given a reminder of the geography topics they have studied during the term. This could take many different forms, including:

- a PowerPoint presentation with images to represent the topics studied

- a mind-map showing the principal content areas

- a table of topics built up by asking pupils to identify subject matter studied during the year.

Activities

🄴 Favourite topics

Pair the pupils up with a learning partner and ask them to tell their partner what their three favourite topics have been in geography over the last term. They should explain why they have enjoyed these topics the most. Then swap roles and repeat the exercise.

Ⓜ Geography poster

Ask the pupils to identify between three and five really interesting things they have learnt in geography this year and turn them into a poster suitable for displaying around school when options choices are being made.

Ⓒ The same and different

Organise the pupils to work in groups of four. They should take it in turns to tell the others in the group what their favourite geography topics of the last school year have been. What are the similarities between the views of their group and what are the differences? Can they explain these?

Teacher's tips

- To help your pupils understand what it required of them, they would benefit from seeing examples of work produced by other pupils working on the above tasks in previous years.

- If any of your pupils are struggling to identify *multiple* topics that they have enjoyed (hopefully there will be very few such pupils!), ask them to explain in more detail the aspects of their favoured subjects that they have enjoyed, or the precise reasons for their selections.

- This task is likely to yield a considerable amount of material that is useful as promotional matter for geography as an option choice. Make sure you make the most of this material through displays around school, articles in your school magazine/newsletter and features on your school website.

Extension

It is important that your pupils get into the habit of systematically reviewing their learning in geography, including the degree to which they have enjoyed different aspects of the course. The above activities should help your pupils to develop the confidence to speak to their peers and teachers about their levels of enjoyment of the course. The tasks will also encourage pupils to routinely review their enjoyment of learning in future.

The activities could also provide the springboard for pupil input to a range of publicity and marketing materials for the geography department, in particular your school prospectus.

More reflection on your geography course

Main topic: Reflection on learning.

Key geographical question: What have you learnt on your geography course over the last term?

This is another self-contained synoptic activity that can be carried out at the beginning or end of a lesson. Like the activity 'Reflecting on your geography course' (see page 159), the following activity needs to be carried out towards the end of a term, or at least the end of a discrete learning unit, to allow pupils to look back and make overall comments about their learning. The activity aims to help pupils be more reflective about their learning and pick out what they consider to be the most important knowledge or skills they have learnt during a period of study.

This is another activity that is intended to be used either as a starter or a plenary, and can be equally powerful in either context.

Starter/plenary

Pupil stimulus

This activity requires some preparation by your pupils as they need to have access to their geography books/folders to do the activity properly – these are the main stimuli for this activity. Additional stimulus material should be provided to give pupils a complete overview of the topics studied during the review period; this could take a variety of forms in order to be accessible to pupils with different learning preferences (e.g. a mind-map; photo-montage; list of topics; video clips of key topics; books covering some of the principal topics etc.).

Activities
❺ Important learning

Ask the pupils to imagine that they are going to have a chat with a parent or other relative about their geography course. Ask them to write down three important things that they think they have learnt on the course this term and for each explain why they think it is important.

Ⓜ Five significant things

Ask the pupils to make a list of five significant things they have learnt over the last term in geography and explain why they have chosen each one. They should then swap their answers with a learning partner.

Ⓒ Ten noteworthy things

Ask the pupils to identify up to ten noteworthy things (knowledge or skills) that they have learnt over the last term in geography, and make a careful note of these. Then they should consider the degree to which each of these could make a genuine contribution to improving the quality of life for people in the UK or overseas.

Teacher's tips

- The degree to which your pupils are able to review their own learning will depend on their prior experience in this area, which can vary from school to school and even between different departments within a school. They *may* need considerable support in this area, including examples to explain how geography pupils might identify the most significant learning over a term.

- This is a classic example of an activity with no 'right' answer, as your pupils are communicating their personal views on the most important things they have learnt over the previous term – and these will clearly vary from one pupil to another. Some pupils feel uneasy when there is no right answer to work towards and may need reassurance that their own views are just as valid as another pupil's.

- This type of synoptic review work is easier to carry out if your pupils are already accustomed to reviewing their learning at the end of shorter learning periods – in particular individual lessons. For this reason you should make sure that *end of lesson* learning reviews are an integral part of your geography curriculum.

Extension

Although your pupils may initially find writing learning reviews rather challenging, they are an important way of keeping your pupils engaged in their learning and therefore should be built into the final week of each term. When your pupils leave you – be that in Year 9, 11 or 13 – they can use their termly reviews to produce a small illustrated booklet summarising their overall learning on the geography course.

Adventurous teachers may wish to take things further by getting pupils to review other aspects of their geography course, in particular the quality of *teaching* they have experienced. This is a very enriching experience for all concerned, and will help you to fine-tune your teaching so it engages and stimulates a wider range of pupils.